Mastering Apache Pulsar

Cloud Native Event Streaming at Scale

Jowanza Joseph

Beijing · Boston · Farnham · Sebastopol · Tokyo

Mastering Apache Pulsar

by Jowanza Joseph

Published by O'Reilly Media, Inc., 1005 Gravenstein Highway North, Sebastopol, CA 95472.

O'Reilly books may be purchased for educational, business, or sales promotional use. Online editions are also available for most titles (*http://oreilly.com*). For more information, contact our corporate/institutional sales department: 800-998-9938 or *corporate@oreilly.com*.

Acquisitions Editor: Jessica Haberman
Development Editor: Angela Rufino
Production Editor: Christopher Faucher
Copyeditor: Audrey Doyle
Proofreader: Tom Sullivan

Indexer: Judith McConville
Interior Designer: David Futato
Cover Designer: Karen Montgomery
Illustrator: Kate Dullea

December 2021:   First Edition

Revision History for the First Edition
2021-12-06:   First Release

See *http://oreilly.com/catalog/errata.csp?isbn=9781492084907* for release details.

978-1-492-08490-7

[LSI]

Table of Contents

Preface

Why I Wrote This Book

Throughout my career, I've been tasked with learning complex systems as part of my job. Early on I had to learn how to write MapReduce jobs and understand the intricacies of the Hadoop Distributed File System (HDFS) and the Hadoop ecosystem; years later I learned early versions of Apache Spark. Today I'm still tasked with learning about complex systems for my job. Over the years, well-written technical blog posts, articles, and books have been instrumental in my ability to learn and to apply what I learn at work. With this book, I sought to create a resource that would provide a thorough explanation of the value of Apache Pulsar which could be long-lasting and fun.

Along with Apache Pulsar as a technology with its trade-offs and consideration is a broader ecosystem and ideas of event streaming. This book provides a nurturing environment to work through the event streams paradigm and provide the reader with context and a road map for adopting event streaming architectures.

Who This Book Is For

This book is targeted at two audiences: those who want to learn about Apache Pulsar and those who are curious about event streaming architectures. For the first audience, this book provides a thorough overview of Apache Pulsar, all of its components, and code samples for getting started with Pulsar and its ecosystem. For the second audience, it serves as a primer for adding Apache Pulsar, Apache Kafka, or another event streaming technology to your architecture.

How I Organized This Book

I spend Chapters 1 through 3 explaining the motivation for Apache Pulsar and the rise of event streams, as well as provide the reader with more supporting content. In Chapters 4 through 10, I dive deep into the internals of Pulsar, component by component, to give the reader a complete understanding of how Pulsar works. I finish the book by focusing on the operational considerations of Pulsar. Chapters 11 and 12 take a detailed look at deploying Pulsar and operating Pulsar in production. These chapters dive deeper into what Pulsar looks like when deployed on systems like Kubernetes and what metrics are available for use as an operator. In Chapter 13, I imagine what the future of Pulsar will look like in 3–5 years, including ways the project can expand to meet the growing needs of the community. Finally, Appendices A through D cover topics like Admin APIs, Security, and GeoReplication. I believe that organizing the book in this way will give the reader the best experience reading the book end to end as well as using it as a reference manual if needed.

Conventions Used in This Book

The following typographical conventions are used in this book:

Italic
  Indicates new terms, URLs, email addresses, filenames, and file extensions.

`Constant width`
  Used for program listings, as well as within paragraphs to refer to program elements such as variable or function names, databases, data types, environment variables, statements, and keywords.

`Constant width bold`
  Shows commands or other text that should be typed literally by the user.

`Constant width italic`
  Shows text that should be replaced with user-supplied values or by values determined by context.

Using Code Examples

Supplemental material (code examples, exercises, etc.) is available for download at *http://www.github.com/josep2*.

If you have a technical question or a problem using the code examples, please send email to *bookquestions@oreilly.com*.

This book is here to help you get your job done. In general, if example code is offered with this book, you may use it in your programs and documentation. You do not need to contact us for permission unless you're reproducing a significant portion of the code. For example, writing a program that uses several chunks of code from this book does not require permission. Selling or distributing examples from O'Reilly books does require permission. Answering a question by citing this book and quoting example code does not require permission. Incorporating a significant amount of example code from this book into your product's documentation does require permission.

We appreciate, but generally do not require, attribution. An attribution usually includes the title, author, publisher, and ISBN. For example: "*Mastering Apache Pulsar* by Jowanza Joseph (O'Reilly). Copyright © 2022 Jowanza Joseph, 978-1-492-08490-7."

If you feel your use of code examples falls outside fair use or the permission given above, feel free to contact us at *permissions@oreilly.com*.

O'Reilly Online Learning

 For more than 40 years, *O'Reilly Media* has provided technology and business training, knowledge, and insight to help companies succeed.

Our unique network of experts and innovators share their knowledge and expertise through books, articles, and our online learning platform. O'Reilly's online learning platform gives you on-demand access to live training courses, in-depth learning paths, interactive coding environments, and a vast collection of text and video from O'Reilly and 200+ other publishers. For more information, visit *http://oreilly.com*.

How to Contact Us

Please address comments and questions concerning this book to the publisher:

O'Reilly Media, Inc.
1005 Gravenstein Highway North
Sebastopol, CA 95472
800-998-9938 (in the United States or Canada)
707-829-0515 (international or local)
707-829-0104 (fax)

We have a web page for this book, where we list errata, examples, and any additional information. You can access this page at *https://oreil.ly/mastering-apache-pulsar*.

Email *bookquestions@oreilly.com* to comment or ask technical questions about this book.

For news and information about our books and courses, visit *http://oreilly.com*.

Find us on Facebook: *http://facebook.com/oreilly*

Follow us on Twitter: *http://twitter.com/oreillymedia*

Watch us on YouTube: *http://youtube.com/oreillymedia*

Acknowledgments

First, I want to thank the creators and maintainers of the open source Apache Pulsar project. Their work brought the project to fruition, and without it, this book would not exist. I also want to thank the editorial and content acquisition teams at O'Reilly. They challenged me to make this book as good as possible, and it would only be a fraction as good without their work. I would also like to thank my wife, Bethany. She provided all the illustrations for this book and supported me through the year I spent writing it. Finally, I'd like to thank the technical editors who provided the invaluable feedback that made this book possible.

## CHAPTER 1

The Value of Real-Time Messaging

Real-time messaging systems power many of the systems we rely on today for banking, food, transportation, internet service, and communication, among others. They provide the infrastructure to make many of the daily interactions we have with these systems seem like magic. Apache Pulsar is one of these real-time messaging systems, and throughout this book, we'll dig into what makes it unique. But first we'll discuss the motivation for building systems like Pulsar so that you have some context for why we would take on the complexity of a real-time system with all of its moving parts.

Data in Motion

When I was 11 years old, I started a small business selling trading cards in my school cafeteria. The business model was simple: I bought packs of Pokémon cards, figured out which ones were the most valuable through cross-checking on internet forums, and then attempted to sell them to other kids during lunch break. What started as an exciting and profitable venture soon turned into a crowded space with many other children entering the market and trying to make some spending money of their own. My daily take-home profit dropped from about $1 to 25 cents, and I thought about quitting the business. I talked to my stepfather about it one evening over dinner, looking for advice from someone who ran a small business too (although one that was much more profitable than mine). After listening to me intently, he absorbed what I said and took a deep breath. He explained that I needed a competitive advantage, something that would make me stick out in a space that was crowded with many other kids. I asked him what kinds of things would give me a competitive advantage, and he chuckled. He told me I needed to figure it out myself, and that when I did, I should come back and talk to him.

For weeks I puzzled over what I could be doing differently. Day after day I watched other children transact in the school cafeteria, and nothing came to me immediately. One day I talked to my friend Edgar, who watched all the Pokémon card transactions more intently than I did. I asked him what he was looking at, and he explained that he was keeping track of all the cards sold that day. He walked from table to table, holding a ledger (see Figure 1-1) and recording all the transactions he witnessed. Edgar let me look through his notebook, and I saw weeks' worth of Pokémon card transactions. That's when it dawned on me that I could use the data he collected to augment my selling strategy and figure out where there was an unmet demand for cards! I told Edgar to meet me after school to talk about the next steps and a business partnership.

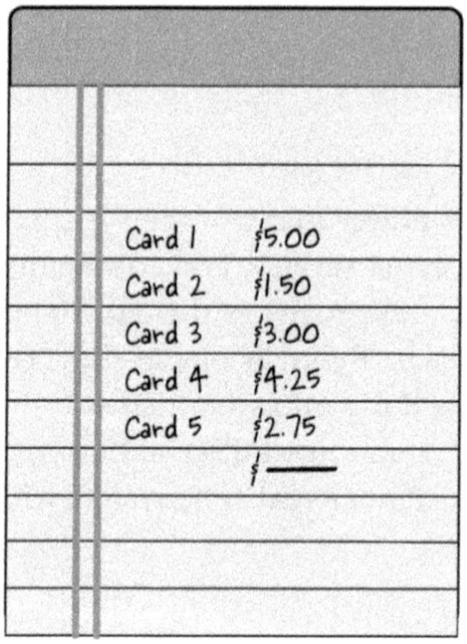

Figure 1-1. Edgar's ledger included the price of each card sold.

When school was out, Edgar and I met and came up with a game plan. I pulled out all of my cards, and we went through them and painstakingly created an inventory sheet. I cross-referenced my inventory with the sales Edgar had collected in his notebook. With this information, I felt confident we could be competitive with the other kids and undercut them where it made sense. Thanks to our new inventory and pricing model, Edgar and I spent the next three weeks selling lots of cards and making some money. But although during that time our daily profit slowly rose from 25 cents to around 50 cents, we still weren't making my original profit of $1 per day, and now we had to share the revenues, which meant we were working much harder and making less money. We decided something had to give, and there had to be another way to make this process easier.

When Edgar and I talked about the limitations of our business, one aspect stuck out. There were only two of us, but there were five tables where kids sold Pokémon cards. Frequently, we would begin selling at the wrong table. Our cards were not the cards the kids at the table wanted to buy. We would miss out on the market opportunity for the day, and often for a week or more, while waiting for new customers. We needed a way to be at all five tables at once. Furthermore, we needed a way to communicate with each other in real time across the tables. Edgar and I schemed for a few days and came up with the plan depicted in Figure 1-2.

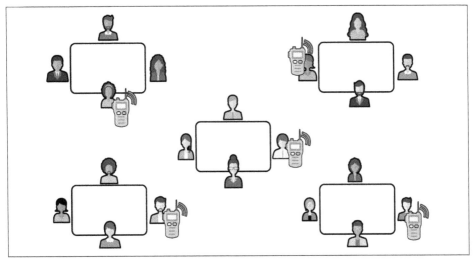

Figure 1-2. A diagram of our card-selling scheme. At each table, one member of our company had a walkie-talkie and we communicated the prices of transactions to one other over the walkie-talkie.

We recruited three other students who were trying to break into the Pokémon card-selling market. We split the cards we wanted to sell evenly among the five of us, and each of us went to one of the five cafeteria tables attempting to sell the cards in our hand. Each of us also had a notebook and a walkie-talkie. When one of us overheard another kid negotiating the sale of one of their cards, that person would communicate the information to the other four in our group. We would all keep the same ledger of prices, and if someone in our group had the card of interest, the person at that table would offer it to the buyer at a lower price. With this strategy, we could always undercut the competition, and all five of us had a picture of the Pokémon card market for that day. Thanks to the new company strategy, our Pokémon card profits rose from 50 cents a day to $2.50 a day. Our teachers eventually shut down the business, and I haven't sold Pokémon cards since.

This story illustrates the value of data in motion. Before we began collecting and broadcasting the Pokémon card sales, the data had little value. It did not have a material impact on our ability to sell cards. Our walkie-talkies and ledgers were a simple system that enabled us to communicate bids and asks in real time across the entire market. Armed with that information, we could make informed decisions about our inventory and sell more cards than we were able to before. While our real-time system only enriched me by a few quarters a day, the system's principles enable rich experiences throughout modern life.

Resource Efficiency

In my trading card business, one of the company's significant advantages was the ability to collect data once and share it with everyone in the company. That ability enabled us to take advantage of sales at the cafeteria tables. In other words, it gave each person at a table a global outlook. This global outlook decentralized the information about sales and created redundancy in our network. Commonly, if one member of the crew was writing and missed an update, they could ask everyone else in the company what their current state of affairs was and they would be able to update their outlook.

While my trading card business was small and inconsequential in the larger scheme of things, resource efficiency can be a boon for companies of any size. When you consider modern enterprise, many events happen that have downstream consequences. Consider the simple meetings that every company has. Creating a calendar meeting requires scheduling time on multiple people's calendars, reserving a room, setting up videoconferencing software, and often, ordering refreshments for attendees. With tools like Google Calendar, we can schedule a meeting with multiple people and coordinate it by simply clicking a few buttons and entering some information into a form (see Figure 1-3). Once that event is created, emails are sent, calendars are tentatively booked, pizza is ordered, and the room is reserved.

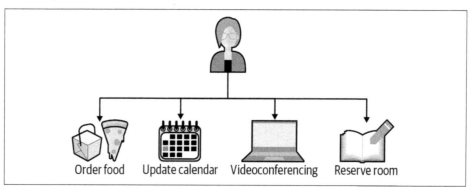

Figure 1-3. With event-driven architectures, complex tasks like scheduling meeting invites across multiple participants become much easier.

Without the platforms to manage and choreograph the calendar invite, administrative overhead can grow like a tumor. Administrators would have to make phone calls, collect RSVPs, and put a sticky note on the door of a conference room. Real-time systems provide value in other systems we use every day, from customer relationship management (CRM) to payroll systems.

Interesting Applications

Resource efficiency is one reason to utilize a messaging system, but an enhanced user experience may ultimately be a more compelling reason. While the software we use serves a utilitarian purpose, enhancing the user experience can make it easier to complete our intended task as well as new and unintended tasks. The user experience can be enhanced through several methods. The most notable are 1) improving the design to make interfaces easier to navigate and 2) doing more on behalf of the user. Exploring the second of these methods, programs that perform on the user's behalf can quickly and accurately take an everyday experience and turn it into something magical. Consider a program that automatically deposits money into your savings account when there is a credit in your checking account. Each time a check clears, the program uses the balance and other contexts regarding the account to deposit a certain amount of money in your savings account. Over time, you save money without ever feeling the pain of saving. Messaging systems are the backbone of systems like this one. In this section we will explore a few examples in more detail and discuss precisely how a messaging platform enables rich user experiences.

Banking

Banks provide the capital that powers much of our economy. To buy a home or car and, in many cases, start a business, you will likely need to borrow money from a bank. If I were to be kind, I would best describe the process of borrowing money from a financial institution as excruciating. In many cases, borrowing money requires that you print out your bank statements so that the bank's loan officers can get an understanding of your monthly expenses. They may also use these printouts to verify your income and tax returns. In many cases, you may provide bank statements, pay stubs, tax returns, and other documents to prequalify for a loan, and then provide the same copies two months later to get the actual loan. While this sounds superfluous in an era of technology, the bank has good reason to be as thorough and intrusive as possible.

For a bank, lending you six figures' worth of money comes at considerable risk. By performing extensive checks on your bank statements and other documents, the bank reduces the risk of approving you for a loan. Banks also face significant regulations, and without a good understanding of your credit, they may face loss of licensing for failing to conduct due diligence. To modernize this credit approval system, we need to look at the problem through a slightly different lens.

When a customer prequalifies for a loan, the bank agrees it will lend up to a certain dollar amount contingent on the applicant having the same creditworthiness when they are ready to act on the loan. Typically, a software system connected to the bank will send notifications to the customer's credit card companies for predetermined events (such as checking a customer's credit). The bank is notified in real time if the customer does anything that will jeopardize the closing of the loan. Also, based on the customer's behavior, the bank can update in real time how much the customer can borrow and have a clear understanding of the probability of a successful close. This end-to-end flow is depicted in Figure 1-4. After the initial data collection for prequalification, a real-time pipeline of transactions and credit card usage is sent to the bank so that there are no surprises.

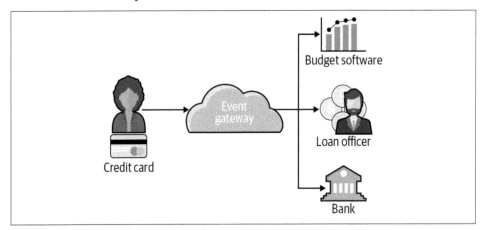

Figure 1-4. Credit card usage and risk are communicated to many downstream consumers.

This process is superior in many ways to the traditional process of completing a full application at both loan preapproval and approval. It reduces the friction of closing the loan (where the bank would make money) and puts the borrower in control. For the financial institution providing the real-time data, it's just a matter of routing data used for another purpose for the lender. The efficiency gained and value provided from this approach is exact.

Medical

Hospitals, medical staff, and medical software are under heightened scrutiny. This scrutiny often looks like compliance and authorization checks by affiliated government entities. When something goes wrong in the medical field, it can be much more devastating than losing money, as with our banking example. Mistakes in the medical field can cause permanent injury or death for a patient, the suspension or revocation of the practitioner's medical license, or a sanction for a hospital. Because of this high level of scrutiny, even a routine visit to a doctor's office can feel slow and inefficient in the best case and extremely frustrating in the worst case. There are many forms to fill out; there is a lot of waiting, and you are often asked the same questions multiple times by different people. Not only does this create inefficiency, it also translates into an expensive doctor's visit.

How would a real-time system help the hospital? Some hospitals in Utah are trying to tackle this problem. The complaints these hospitals heard most often from patients concerned having to give their medical history more than once per visit. When a patient arrived for a visit, they would fill out a form with their health history. When they saw a medical assistant, they were asked many of the same questions they had already answered on the form. When they finally saw their doctor, they were asked the same questions again. The health history provides a reasonable basis for doctors to work from and can prevent common problems concerning misdiagnoses and prescriptions. However, collecting health history often comes at the cost of clinic time, which translates into a poor patient experience and extra work for the staff.

The software engineering department and health providers at these hospitals worked together to reimagine what a health history system should look like. Ultimately, they reengineered the patient record system to make it an event-driven, real-time system. Now when a patient arrives at one of these hospitals, they enter their information on a tablet (see Figure 1-5). The data is saved to the patient record system, and three minutes before the scheduled appointment time the doctor receives a notification to log on and check the patient's information. The doctor uses those three minutes to end the current appointment and start reading the next patient's chart. When the doctor arrives in the patient's room, they know everything they need to start a conversation with the patient about their care.

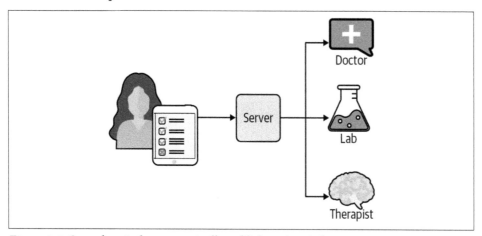

Figure 1-5. Some hospitals automatically publish patient information to necessary parties, providing a better user experience.

After the visit, if the patient needs to have any lab work or other tests performed, the doctor clicks a button and the test order is sent to the lab. Similarly, when the patient checks into the lab, their information is auto-populated. While initially designed to prevent duplication of collecting medical history, the system has had a far-reaching impact. Not only have these hospitals saved money, but the patient experience has improved dramatically.

Security

For governments and private companies, fraud and hacking on the internet are costly problems without a one-size-fits-all solution. The hardest part of fighting hacking and fraud is the number of places or vectors an organization has to protect. Fraud can occur if the bank is unable to verify the identity or authorization of a member accurately (see Figure 1-6). For example, if someone who isn't the owner of an account convinces the bank they are, they can act as the account owner, withdrawing funds, taking out loans, or other nefarious behavior. Hacks can happen when an employee accidentally clicks on a phishing attempt link or an engineer applies the wrong policy to their code (see Figure 1-7). Defending against multiple attack vectors is expensive and requires specialized skills.

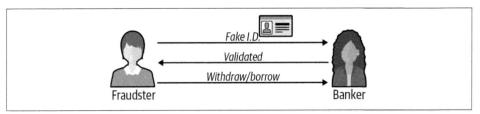

Figure 1-6. A fraudster uses fabricated identification to fool the banker into thinking they are a legitimate client. The fraudster's identity is confirmed and they use this access to legitimately withdraw funds.

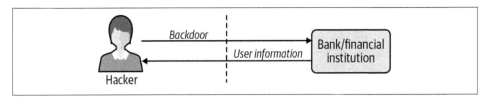

Figure 1-7. A hacker gains entry to a financial institution through a backdoor (unauthorized channel). The hacker uses this backdoor to gain access to user data.

Real-time systems can reduce some of the cost and overhead of protecting an organization against fraud and hacks. Many organizations require a specialized approach to each threat vector they face. They may use one vendor for their firewall, another to protect their email, and a third to manage their cloud computing policies. For many of these vendors, it's not in their business interest to make their security products interoperable with other vendors' products. Many of these vendors use the same data to detect different threats.

Some new product offerings in the market utilize the real-time nature of the data (internet traffic) and provide an all-in-one solution (see Figure 1-8). These offerings treat each new connection as a threat. They use an event-driven system with machine learning, business logic, and other approaches to determine whether a particular request is safe. This approach is also modular, in that the vendor can customize the threat protection for each customer based on their needs. This approach is superior to the alternatives because it reuses data passing through the system and choreographs responses from multiple systems.

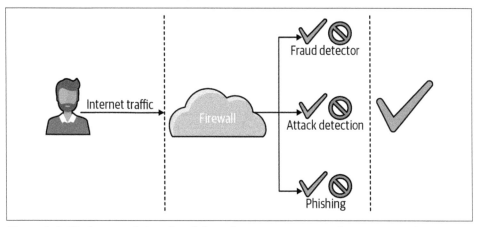

Figure 1-8. Modern, real-time fraud detection systems treat each new connection as a threat.

Internet of Things

The use of smart speakers and other smart-home appliances has been on the rise around the world. With the broader availability of internet service and the lower cost of producing internet-connected devices, many first-time smart-device buyers have entered the market. In general, users of smart devices find utility in what these devices have to offer. I've been a smart-home enthusiast for many years now, and while each camera, sensor, and speaker has utility on its own, the utility they have when working together is hard to rival. Working together takes smart homes from many applications on a smartphone to a holistic system that can meet the user's needs. Unfortunately, getting the devices from myriad manufacturers to work together can be difficult. For the manufacturers, it may not be in their best business interest to make their products interoperable with those of their competitors. There also may be sound technical reasons why a device doesn't support a popular protocol. For a user, these decisions can be limiting and frustrating. I found these limitations too prohibitive and decided to build my own proprietary bridge for use with my consumer-grade smart-home products.

The majority of consumer-grade smart-home devices speak one of three protocols: Bluetooth, WiFi, or Zigbee. Most of us are familiar with Bluetooth; it is a commonly used protocol for connecting devices from computer keyboards and mice to hearing aids. Bluetooth doesn't require any internet connectivity and is widely supported. WiFi is a wireless internet connectivity protocol. Zigbee is a low-energy communication protocol commonly used in smart-home devices.

Suppose you had 20 smart-home devices from different manufacturers, and each spoke either Bluetooth, WiFi, or Zigbee. If you wanted them all to work together to, say, monitor your home, it would not be easy to do. However, if you could build a bridge that would translate WiFi into Zigbee, Zigbee into Bluetooth, and so on, the possibilities would be endless. That's the idea I worked with when designing the smart-home bridge in Figure 1-9.

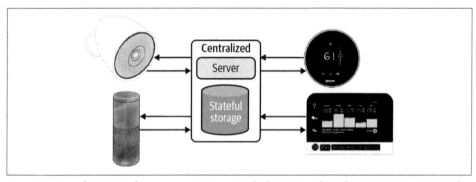

Figure 1-9. A diagram of my smart system. Each device on the edge communicates with a different protocol but publishes its events to a centralized MQTT server which can choreograph the events.

Each of my smart-home devices was event-driven, meaning that when an event occurred that was important to the device, the device would publish the event to a centralized server. For all the smart-home devices I owned, I could tap into their software and broadcast that same event to my event bridge. I use MQTT (Message Queuing Telemetry Transport), a lightweight messaging system designed for Internet of Things applications. Now, whenever an event occurs in my home (like a door opening), it will publish natively to the manufacturer's platform as well as to my platform. I built a small event-processing platform that takes events posted to MQTT and performs actions when predefined criteria are met. For example, if a door opens but doesn't close within two minutes, it will send a push notification to my wife. Or if the alarm system is armed and it detects someone is home, it will delay notification for a few seconds.

My smart-home system provides much more utility to me now that all the events are codified in a reusable way. That is the power of real time, and it's also the power of event-driven architectures.

Summary

In this chapter we explored examples of real-time and event-oriented systems in the real world. We used these systems to help motivate the need for a system like Apache Pulsar. In the upcoming chapters we'll move from a high-level view of why we need Pulsar to a more detailed view based on programming and systems literature as well as real-world examples.

## CHAPTER 2

Event Streams and Event Brokers

Event streams and event brokers are at the heart of every real-time system. An *event stream* is an endless series of events. Let's revisit the banking example in Chapter 1. A borrower's financial transactions can be considered an event stream. Each time a borrower uses their credit card, applies for a new line of credit, or deposits a check, those actions or events are appended to their event stream. Since the event stream is infinite, the bank can use it to return to any point in the borrower's past. If the bank wanted to know what a borrower's bank account looked like on a specific day in history, it could reconstruct that from an event stream. The event stream is a powerful concept, and when equipped with this data, it can empower organizations and developers to make life-changing experiences.

Event brokers are the technology platforms that store event streams and interact with clients that read data from or write data to event streams. Apache Pulsar is an event broker at heart. However, calling Pulsar *only* an event broker would minimize its scope and impact. To fully understand what makes Pulsar unique, it is beneficial to dive into some of the strengths and weaknesses of event brokers and their approaches to implementing event streams. This chapter will walk through some historical context and motivate a discussion around the need for Apache Pulsar.

Publish/Subscribe

Developers across disciplines in software engineering commonly use the publish/subscribe pattern. At its core, this pattern decouples software systems and smooths the user experience of asynchronous programming. Popular messaging technologies like Apache Pulsar, Apache Kafka, RabbitMQ, NATS, and ActiveMQ all utilize the publish/subscribe pattern in their protocols. It's worth jumping into this pattern's history to understand its significance and build on why Pulsar is unique.

In 1987, Kenneth Birman and Thomas Joseph published a paper titled "Exploiting virtual synchrony in distributed systems" in the *ACM SIGOPS Operating Systems Review*.[1] Their paper describes an early implementation of a large-scale messaging platform built on the publish/subscribe pattern. In their paper, the authors make a convincing case around the publish/subscribe pattern's value. Specifically, they claim that systems implemented this way *feel* synchronous, even though they are inherently asynchronous. To illustrate this point more clearly, let's dive into the publish/subscribe pattern with some examples.

The idea of a subscription is commonplace in the 21st century. I have subscriptions to news services, entertainment, food delivery, loyalty programs, and many others. Figure 2-1 is a simple illustration of a pub/sub pattern. I *subscribe* to goods for services from a retailer or entertainer, and they deliver me goods or services based on an agreement. The news services I subscribe to are the best way to illustrate a publish/subscribe pattern. I subscribe to a news service, and when a news source publishes a new article, I expect to receive it on my phone. In this example, you can consider my news service provider to be an event broker, the news publication to be a producer, and me to be a consumer. There are a few features in this relationship that are worth pointing out.

Figure 2-1. The publish/subscribe pattern decouples software systems and smooths the user experience of asynchronous programming.

First, there is no coupling between the news publication (publisher) and the subscriber (consumer). The news publication does not need to know that I'm a subscriber; they focus on writing articles and sending them to the news service. Similarly, I don't need to know anything about the mechanisms of the news publication; the news service provides a reliable mechanism for publication and consumption. From a consumer perspective, promptly getting news on my phone feels magical. I can control how many messages I receive per day and what times I prefer to receive them. For the news publication, they can focus on producing quality news. Delivering the news to the right customers at the right time is managed by the news service.

The aha moment in the virtual synchrony paper was that the publish/subscribe pattern makes asynchronous workflows feel synchronous. Figure 2-2 depicts this model. Examining the interactions with my news service from all angles, it does feel synchronous. I don't feel like I have to ask and wait for a relationship with my news

---

1 Kenneth Birman and Thomas Joseph, "Exploiting virtual synchrony in distributed systems," *ACM SIGOPS Operating Systems Review 21*, no. 5 (November 1987): 123–138.

publication; it just shows up when I need it. The publisher publishes their stories to the news service, and their stories are in users' hands.

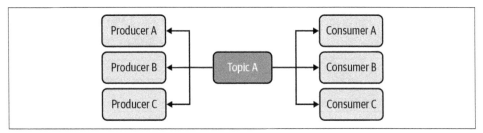

Figure 2-2. In this publish/subscribe topology, there are multiple producers and consumers.

The event stream implements a publish/subscribe pattern, but it has one critical distinction: the event broker must retain the same order for every subscriber. This distinction may not seem like much at first blush, but it enables a whole new way of using the publish/subscribe pattern. Consider our example of the news service. When a new customer signs up for the service, they will receive news articles in the future but likely will not receive all past messages onto their device on sign-up. Most messaging systems guarantee the delivery of a published message to a current subscriber and purposefully release messages that are already delivered. For an event stream, the event broker retains the entire history of data. When a new consumer subscribes to the event stream, they choose where they want to start consuming from (including the beginning of time).

Queues

A queue is a different approach to a publish/subscribe pattern. In the publish/subscribe pattern discussed in the previous section, every subscriber to a topic receives a published message. In the queue model, only one subscriber will receive a message published to a topic. The queue model tackles a specific kind of publish/subscribe problem where each message in the queue is waiting on work to be completed, and the subscribers perform that work. Consider the process of being invited to a party (see Figure 2-3). An invitation to anyone who has access to them is analogous to a queue (left) and an invitation to a specific person is analogous to an event stream (right).

The queue model is more straightforward than the event stream model and works for a larger class of applications in which a client receives a work unit, then publishes the work unit to the messaging system, and a downstream consumer completes the work. Email, unsubscribing, deleting records, orchestration of events, and indexing are examples of this class of applications.

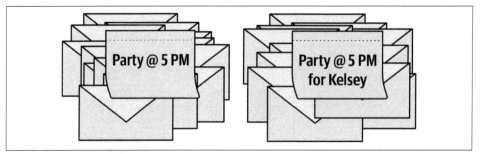

Figure 2-3. A generic invitation is shown on the left and an invitation for a specific invitee (Kelsey) is shown on the right.

Some messaging systems are purpose-built for the queue model. This class of messaging system is called a *work queue*. Work queues are designed for managing the workloads of programmatic processes. They have three purposes: 1) keep track of all the work to be done (a queue); 2) allow the appropriate worker to perform work; and 3) report back their completion (or lack thereof) of work. Beanstalkd is a widely used messaging system that is a work queue. Beanstalkd's design is purposefully simple and doesn't require the user to configure it. Let's walk through an example in some more depth to get a better handle on Beanstalkd and the queue model.

Beanstalkd organizes work into logical lists called tubes. You can think of a tube as a queue; it is an ordered list of work to be completed, and it has a name. Inside a tube is a job; since Beanstalkd is a work queue, most of the language and concepts are aligned with *work*. Beanstalkd has *publishers*, or programmatic clients that are asking for work to be complete, and it has *subscribers*, or programmatic clients that are picking up work and then marking it as complete. Here is a simple Beanstalkd client publishing a new job to the "worka" tube:

```
// A python program that connects to a local instance of Beanstalkd and creates a
// job
import beanstalkc
beanstalk = beanstalkc.Connection(host='localhost', port=14711)
beanstalk.use('worka')
beanstalk.put('my job 123')
```

Now that we've published work, we can connect to the same "worka" tube and complete the work:

```
import beanstalkc

beanstalk = beanstalkc.Connection(host='localhost', port=14711)
beanstalk.use('worka')
job = beanstalk.reserve() // reserves the job in the tube
job.body // prints "my job 123"
job.delete() // Deletes the job from beanstalkd, marking it was complete
```

In this model, the Beanstalkd server is responsible for keeping track of which jobs go to which tubes, but the consumer manages most of the complexity in the system. The consumer is responsible for the following:

- Reserving the work
- Marking the work as complete
- Resubmitting the work if it fails
- Maintaining a connection with Beanstalkd

In Beanstalkd, typically one job goes to one worker (subscriber).[2] When we zoom in on the purpose of the work queue, the decision to have a one-to-one relationship with a job and a consumer (worker) is reasonable. However, there are some implicit side effects of this queue model that we should explore in some more detail to understand the differences.

First, in the queue model (and specifically in the Beanstalkd API), we assume that when a job is complete there is no need for it anymore. In fact, in Beanstalkd, the worker should explicitly delete the job when it's no longer being worked on. Second, there is no order preservation for the jobs. This means there is no guarantee that a job arriving at Beanstalkd would be processed in any specific or consistent order. For some applications it may be necessary to allow multiple subscribers to pick up the same job, and it may also be advantageous to have a way to follow how jobs arrived in the queue from a historical perspective.

Failure Modes

Messaging systems can fail. They can fail to deliver messages to subscribers, they can fail to accept publishers' messages, and they can lose messages in transit. Contingent on the system's design and use, each failure can have varying degrees of severity. If we think back on the email examples earlier in this chapter, failure to deliver email can have a varying degree of severity. If you fail to receive your favorite email newsletter in your inbox on a given day, that is not the end of the world. You may spend your time on other, more fulfilling pursuits in the absence of the newsletter. But if a failure occurs in an ecommerce platform's payment pipeline, and the ecommerce platform uses email messages to create *virtual synchrony*, it can prevent a user from receiving their products in the best case and bankrupt the business in the worst case. It's essential to build a messaging platform that is resistant to failures.

---

2 The Beanstalkd protocol explicitly states that one subscriber should consume a job. However, there are some hacks you can implement to ensure that multiple subscribers consume a job. For example, by simply never deleting a job, you can allow every subscriber to see that job once it's released.

Managing the three failures of message acceptance, message delivery, and message storage requires thoughtful design and wise implementations. We'll discuss how Pulsar tackles these issues in the next chapter.

Push Versus Poll

When a producer publishes a new message to a queue or event stream, the way that message propagates to consumers can vary. The two mechanisms for pushing that message to consumers are pushing and polling.

In the *push* model, the event broker pushes messages to a consumer with some predefined configuration. For example, the broker may have a fixed number of messages per period that it sends to a consumer, or it may have a maximum number of messages queued before it pushes them to the consumer. A majority of messaging systems today use a push mechanism because brokers are eager to move messages off their hands.

In an event system, queued messages have some value, but processing the messages is the system's end goal. By eagerly pushing messages to available consumers, the event broker can rid itself of the responsibility for the message. However, as discussed in "Failure Modes" on page 17, an event broker may try to push a consumer message and the consumer may be unavailable. This failure mode necessitates the event broker to retry or, in the queue case, move the message onto another consumer.

An alternative to the push model is the *poll* model. The poll model requires the consumer to ask the event broker for new messages. The consumer may ask for new messages after a configured time interval or may ask based on a downstream event. The advantage of this model is that the consumer is always ready to receive messages when it asks. The disadvantage is that the consumer may not receive messages on time or receive them at all.

The Need for Pulsar

So far in this chapter we've talked about early systems developed to tackle messaging, and we've touched on systems like RabbitMQ, ActiveMQ, and Apache Kafka. These systems require a nontrivial number of resources to develop and a large community to remain viable in a developer market. Why do we need another one? Apache Pulsar addresses three problems that are not addressed by other event broker technologies:

- Unification of streaming and queues
- Modularity
- Performance

Unification

The event stream requires an ordered sequence for messages. That ordered sequence enables the rich applications described in Chapter 1 and is used in many of the applications you use every day. However, an event stream has specific semantics requiring consumers to manage how they process the stream's events. What if an application doesn't require the use of an ordered sequence? What if each client needed to get the next available event and was not concerned about its place in the stream?

Pulsar allows topics to be either a queue or an event stream, as depicted in Figure 2-4. This flexibility means a Pulsar cluster can provide the platform for all the interactions discussed in this chapter.

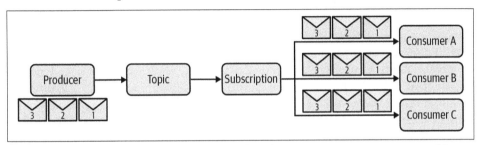

Figure 2-4. In a shared subscription, every subscriber gets every message generated by the producer.

Modularity

We talked about the differences between the queue and event stream models of the publish/subscribe model. While these models differ enough to warrant different architectures, application developers are likely to need both models for building robust software. It's not uncommon for software development teams to use one system intentionally designed for event streams and another for queueing. While this "best tool for the job" approach can be wise, it does have some downsides. One downside is the operational burden of managing two systems. Each system is unique in its maintenance schedule and procedure, best practices, and operations paradigm. An additional downside is that programmers have to familiarize themselves with multiple paradigms and APIs to write applications.

Pulsar is equipped for the queue and event stream models because of its modular design. In Chapter 3, we will walk through all the components of Pulsar in depth, but to motivate this discussion it's worth talking about some of them now. Pulsar's design keeps a clear separation between the various responsibilities of the system.

The following are some of Pulsar's responsibilities:

- Storing data for finite periods for consumers
- Storing data for long periods for consumers
- Ensuring order in the topics

Pulsar's short-term storage is managed by the Pulsar brokers. Pulsar's long-term storage is handled by Apache BookKeeper. These choices enable a rich experience and make Pulsar suitable for a wide range of problems in the messaging space.

For a mature company, migrating from an existing messaging system like RabbitMQ, MQTT, or Kafka to Pulsar may be infeasible. Each of these platforms has a unique protocol, requires custom client libraries, and has a unique paradigm and vernacular. The process of migrating may take years for a sufficiently large organization. Fortunately, Pulsar can be used concurrently with these existing messaging systems, allowing organizations to use, say, Pulsar and RabbitMQ at the same time and slowly migrate their RabbitMQ topics to Pulsar, or keep both running side by side through the Pulsar bridge framework.[3] The Pulsar bridge framework provides a mechanism to translate messages from AMQP 0.9.1 (the protocol RabbitMQ uses) to Pulsar. In this model, the RabbitMQ applications can continue to use RabbitMQ and their AMQP 0.9.1 messages will convert to Pulsar protocol messages in the background. When the team is ready, they can start to consume their RabbitMQ messages from Pulsar where they left off.

The power of Pulsar's modular design is also evident in its ecosystem. Pulsar supports Functions as a Service (see Figure 2-5), as well as the ability to use SQL with Pulsar topic data and change data capture (CDC) with minimal configuration. Each of these features provides additional building blocks and tools for creating rich, event-driven applications.

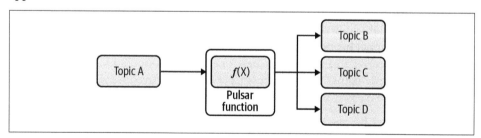

Figure 2-5. Pulsar Functions are a built-in runtime for stream processing in Pulsar.

---

3 We will cover Pulsar bridges in Chapter 12.

Performance

Thus far, we have discussed three critical components of a quality event broker. The broker needs to 1) reliably store data, 2) reliably deliver messages to consumers, and 3) quickly consume messages from publishers. Performing these three tasks well requires thoughtful design and optimized resource utilization. All event brokers have to work through the same disk speed, CPU, memory, and network limitations. In further chapters, we'll get into more detail around the design considerations in Apache Pulsar, but for now let's take a look at how some of them enable exceptional performance and scalability.

In "Modularity" on page 19, we discussed Pulsar's modular approach to storage by using Apache BookKeeper. We focused on how this choice enables features to archive and retrieve Pulsar data. Pulsar administrators can grow the size of the BookKeeper cluster separately from the Pulsar event broker nodes. The storage needs may change during a day, month, or year within a messaging platform. Pulsar enables the flexibility to scale up storage more comfortably with this design decision. When it comes to reliability concerns about storing data, the storage systems' scalability is a significant factor.

Reliability in the consumption of messages is contingent on the event broker being able to consume the volume of messages sent its way. If an event broker can't keep up with the volume of messages, many failure scenarios may follow. Clients connect to Pulsar via the Pulsar protocol and connect to a Pulsar node. Since Pulsar nodes can scale separately from the BookKeeper cluster, scaling up consumption is also more flexible.

Finally, what about raw performance? How many messages can a Pulsar cluster consume per second? How many can it securely store in the BookKeeper cluster per second? There are many published benchmarks[4] on Apache Pulsar and its performance, but you should take every benchmark with a grain of salt. As mentioned earlier in this chapter, every messaging system has constraints. The engineers who design these systems take advantage of their unique knowledge and circumstances. Therefore, designing benchmarks that fairly assess the performance of each platform is often an exercise in futility. That said, Apache Pulsar has a reputation for being a performant platform, and hundreds of companies have chosen Pulsar to manage their event streaming platforms.

---

4 For example, see *Benchmarking Apache Kafka, Apache Pulsar, and RabbitMQ: Which Is the Fastest?* (*https://oreil.ly/b67QJ*); *Benchmarking Pulsar and Kafka—A More Accurate Perspective on Pulsar's Performance* (*https://oreil.ly/uewER*); and *Performance Comparison Between Apache Pulsar and Kafka: Latency* (*https://oreil.ly/u4DpP*).

Summary

In this chapter you acquired the foundational knowledge needed to understand Pulsar's value proposition and uniqueness. From here, we'll pull apart all of Pulsar's components to gain a deep understanding of the basic building blocks. With that knowledge, you'll be ready to dive deep into the APIs and start building applications.

## CHAPTER 3

Pulsar

In Chapter 2, we discussed the motivation for a system like Apache Pulsar: namely, a system that handles both the event stream and pub/sub patterns seamlessly. I provided sufficient evidence for the utility of a system like Pulsar and provided a historical backdrop for asynchronous messaging. We did not, however, cover how Pulsar came into existence. To begin this chapter on the design principles and use cases for Pulsar, it's worth understanding how exactly the system came to be.

Origins of Pulsar

In 2013, Yahoo! reported having 800 million active users across its services. At the time, Yahoo! provided services for email, photo storage, news, social media, chat, and fantasy sports, among others. From an infrastructure perspective, Yahoo! felt it needed to address some of its underlying architecture decisions to meet users' demands and continue to build its world-class services. The messaging architecture used at Yahoo! was thought to be the most important area for improvement. In the company's service-oriented architecture, the messaging system helped all components scale and provided the low-latency primitives to simplify scalability across all services (see Figure 3-1). Following are the most critical aspects for the new messaging platform to meet:

Flexibility
    Yahoo! worked with queues, publish/subscribe, and streaming, and wanted its messaging platform to handle these use cases seamlessly.

Reliability
    Yahoo! was accustomed to 99.999% reliability, and the new system had to have the same level of reliability, if not better.

Performance

Yahoo! needed low, end-to-end latencies for services like chat and email as well as its ad platform.

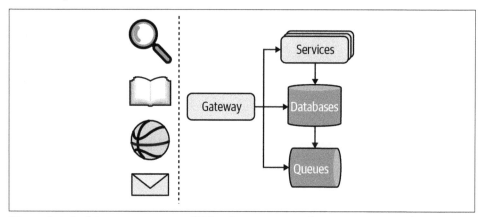

Figure 3-1. In this representation of Yahoo! services, search, news, sports, and email are supported by backend infrastructure, including services, databases, and queues.

Yahoo! evaluated existing messaging technologies and determined that none of the open source or off-the-shelf solutions would work for its scale and needs. Yahoo! decided to create a system to meet its needs and designed and built the first version of Pulsar.

In 2015, Yahoo! deployed its first Pulsar cluster. Pulsar's use quickly exploded to replace the company's existing messaging infrastructure. In 2017, Yahoo! made Pulsar an open source project by donating it to the Apache Software Foundation.

Pulsar Design Principles

Pulsar was designed from the ground up to be the default messaging platform at Yahoo! As Yahoo! is a large technology company with hundreds of millions of users and numerous popular services, using one platform to meet everyone's needs was complicated at best. Scalability and usability challenges were only the tip of the iceberg. At the dawn of Pulsar's design and implementation, many companies were utilizing the public cloud, but cloud adoption was nowhere near what it is today. Creating a system that meets a company's needs today but doesn't lock the company into a single development pattern for years to come is a challenge few engineering teams can meet.

To meet these challenges, the Pulsar designers focused on two essential design principles:

- Modularity
- Performance

Modularity and performance are a rare combination in systems. Like a Thoroughbred made of Legos (see Figure 3-2), Pulsar allows for extensions while never compromising on performance. From these two design principles, some of Pulsar's elegance and foresight come to the surface: namely, its multitenancy, geo-replication, performance, and modularity. We'll dive into each and show how it relates to Pulsar's design principles.

Figure 3-2. The two design principles behind Pulsar are modularity (represented by the Legos) and performance (represented by the Thoroughbred).

Multitenancy

When I was growing up, I lived in an apartment complex with 27 units in a five-story building. We all shared the utilities, including heat, water, cable, and gas. Trying to ensure a suitable temperature, good water pressure, a reliable cable signal, and adequate gas for all the units was impossible. In the winter, the top floor was 75°F (too hot) and the first floor was 65°F (barely tolerable). In the morning, tenants raced to get to the shower before all the hot water was used and the water pressure was low. If several tenants were watching Monday Night Football, it would be difficult to get a reliable signal.

Our apartment complex was multitenant (see Figure 3-3) in that each unit contained its own family but all units shared resources. In software, multitenant systems are designed to run workloads for different customers on the same hardware. Pulsar's flexible subscription model and decoupled architecture enable a high-quality, multitenant experience.

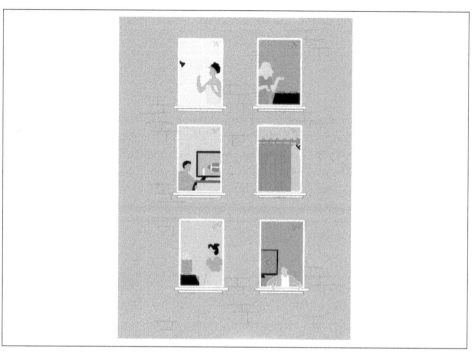

Figure 3-3. In this apartment building, multiple tenants share resources. Without smart management of these resources, one tenant can impact the others. Pulsar's multitenant architecture enables the use of multiple tenants on fixed resources.

Pulsar handles multitenancy through namespacing and allows tenant scheduling on a specific part of the Pulsar cluster. A *namespace* is simply a logical grouping of topics. Namespaces give structure to Pulsar by providing some organizing fabric to the topics. These two mechanisms put the Pulsar cluster operator in full control of resource allocation and isolation for specific tenants. Returning to the example of my apartment building, Pulsar allows a cluster operator to keep together those tenants who like to keep their unit at the same temperature, and to separate those tenants who take showers around the same time to preserve hot water and water pressure. We'll explore multitenancy in Pulsar further in Chapter 4.

Geo-Replication

Yahoo!, a globally distributed company, had more than 800 million users at its peak. Pulsar's usage spread throughout Yahoo! and around the globe, and with that expansion came the responsibility of replicating data. Replication is the process of copying data from one node in Pulsar to another. Replication is a core aspect of two important concepts: performance and redundancy. It's worth taking a moment to consider why these two aspects are important.

We use computers to perform tasks like word processing, browsing the internet, editing photos, and playing games, to name a few. Our computers use software and a few hardware components to make these experiences possible. As we use our computers, we quickly learn their limitations. We may notice that when we have 20 tabs open in our browser, everything on the computer slows down. We may notice we can't process a 4K video and stream a movie concurrently. Every computer has a finite set of hardware resources and a quantifiable limit that the hardware can achieve.

When you consider a system like Apache Pulsar, it runs on hardware that is not dissimilar from your personal computer. The hardware has the same memory, processing power, disk space, network speed, and other limitations of a personal computer. When you consider how to get more power out of your computer, you have a few options:

- Make the programs perform better, given your hardware constraints.
- Get a computer with more hardware to meet your requirements.
- Find a clever way to get more hardware.

The first option is likely already considered and in place. For most of the software we use, like web browsers, email clients, and games, the developers of the software focused on getting the maximum performance from the hardware. Getting a bigger, better computer may be feasible for some budgets, but your needs might quickly outstrip your budget. The clever way to get more hardware is to distribute the needs of our computing system across many computers. This distributed approach to managing hardware requirements is how Pulsar deals with the performance aspect of its responsibilities.

In Figure 3-4, we have three nodes, labeled N_0, N_1, and N_2. Each is able to handle a specific amount of load from an external process. The smallest load that can be managed is 100 MBps and the largest is 2 GBps. Suppose now that the cost of increasing performance by 100 MBps was exponential. This would mean that as you approach 2 GBps and then 3 GBps, you are paying 10 times more than what you were paying at 100 MBps.

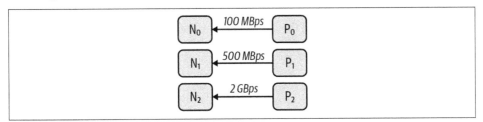

Figure 3-4. Nodes with fixed performance bandwidths ranging from 100 MBps to 2 GBps. To scale the system to ingest more data per second we must add another node of the same size.

Now consider Figure 3-5. In this figure, we have nodes labeled N_0–N_6; all have the constraint of 100 MBps, but instead of one node we have seven nodes. If we can effectively split our tasks in a way that can maximize the throughput of each node, we can get the outcomes we want without running into prohibitively expensive costs. So far, all of the drawings of Pulsar have multiple instances of Pulsar, and that is intentional. It is for performance and cost management, but also for redundancy, which we'll talk about next.

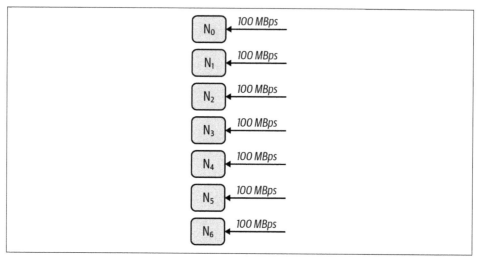

Figure 3-5. Seven nodes, each with a bandwidth of 100 MBps. In this configuration, all the data in the system is split across the seven nodes.

For a third option, consider Figure 3-6. In this figure we have two nodes. N_0 contains all the data entries in an encyclopedia, from A to Z. When someone wants to look up a term, the term is retrieved from N_0 at a specific speed. Notice that N_0 has a fixed disk size of 1 TB. If the encyclopedia requires more than 1 TB of space, we will have to move to another node. The other node, N_1, has the same considerations as N0 but more disk space and can take on more capacity. Both N_0 and N_1 have one critical problem, though: if either of them goes offline, no encyclopedia data can be retrieved. Also, their capacities are fixed, so regardless of what words users are interested in looking up, the nodes contain all the data, useful or not.

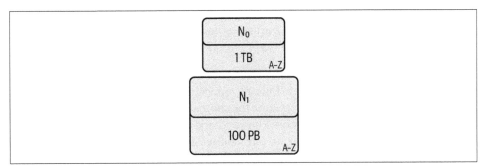

Figure 3-6. Nodes with different configurations but the same encyclopedia requirements. N_1 can store a much larger corpus than N_0.

In Figure 3-7, we see a different model for the encyclopedia. Now, not only are there multiple nodes (N_0–N_3), but none of them contains the entire encyclopedia; rather, only specific letters. This figure also introduces the concept of a coordinator, which will map a request to the right encyclopedia. In this model we get higher throughput, assuming an even distribution of requests across the encyclopedia. One more step would be to have more than one node share their letters. This way, if an individual node is offline, we can still serve requests for those letters in the encyclopedia.

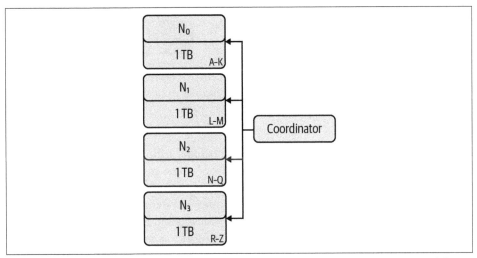

Figure 3-7. A coordinator with distributed workloads. The coordinator is aware of the responsibility of each node, and as it receives new work, it knows where it should be routed.

For Apache Pulsar, both the performance and redundancy considerations of being distributed are fully realized. To build on this further, Pulsar enables distribution across datacenters. In fact, it can be deployed across multiple datacenters by default. This means that, as an application scales across geographies, it can use one Pulsar cluster. Topics are replicated across datacenters, and topic redundancy can be configured to the needs of the applications utilizing the topic. For a topic deployed across hundreds of datacenters around the world, Pulsar manages the complexity of routing data to the right place.

Later in the book, we'll explore how Pulsar's replication protocol works and how replication enables smooth global operations for companies like Splunk. For the remainder of this chapter, we'll focus on how Pulsar components are modular, allowing for a cluster across the globe to appear as one connected cluster (see Figure 3-8). This design and implementation detail separates Pulsar from other systems.

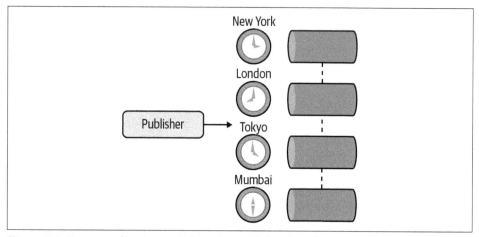

Figure 3-8. In geo-replication in Pulsar, the publisher (producer) sends a message to the brokers, which replicate the messages across geographies as needed.

Performance

As a messaging system, Pulsar's primary responsibility is to reliably and quickly consume publishers' messages and deliver subscribers' messages. Fulfilling these responsibilities on top of being a reliable message storage mechanism is complicated. From the outset, Yahoo! was concerned about building a system with low latency. In its 2016 post "Open-Sourcing Pulsar, Pub-Sub Messaging at Scale" (*https://oreil.ly/Xu0az*), Yahoo! cites average publish latencies of 5 ms as being a strict requirement when building Pulsar. Let's put this into perspective.

One millisecond is one one-thousandth of a second, and the speed of a human eye blink ranges from 100 to 400 milliseconds. Yahoo! required speeds much faster than the blink of an eye just to publish latencies, or the speed at which the message broker receives, saves, and acknowledges the message. Why is this? As I stated earlier, message platforms are often the center of company operations. Publishing to the messaging system is Step 1 among many other steps, but getting safely and quickly to the messaging system is perhaps the most important goal. By ensuring quick publishing times, every other downstream action can begin, and the overall time from when a message was created to when it delivered value is shortened.

While this book covers all of Pulsar's features, building blocks, and ecosystem, the reality is that Pulsar's core functionality is unquestionably fast message delivery. All other features in Pulsar build off of this fundamental truth.

Modularity

At its core, Pulsar's implementation is a distributed log. The distributed log is an excellent primitive for a system like Pulsar because it provides the building blocks for many systems, including databases and file systems. In 2013, Jay Kreps, then a principal staff engineer at LinkedIn, published a blog post titled "The Log: What every software engineer should know about real-time data's unifying abstraction" (*https://oreil.ly/QF0K0*). In this post, Kreps argues that the log provides some key tenants, allowing it to be a building block for real-time systems. Namely, logs are *append only* (meaning you can add to the log but not remove an item from the log) and are indexed based on the order an item was inserted into the log.

Chapter 4 describes Pulsar's implementation of a distributed log in more detail. For now, we'll focus on how building this core enables other messaging models to work with Pulsar.

In Chapter 2 we talked about event streams. An event stream has a one-to-one relationship with a log. Each event is appended to the stream and ordered by an index (offset). When a consumer publishes an event stream, maintaining the order in which the messages were published is vital. Pulsar's event-based implementation works well for this use case. For a queue, the order in which the messages are published doesn't matter. Additionally, the queue consumers don't care where they are relative to the queue's beginning or end. In this instance, you can still use the log but relax some of the constraints to model a queue.

Alternative pub/sub implementations can be small moderations on top of a distributed log implementation. For example, MQTT (Message Queuing Telemetry Transport) is implemented in Pulsar via the MQTT-On-Pulsar project. Other implementations and protocols can run on top of Pulsar with modifications to the core log, such as the Kafka protocol or the AMQP 1.0 protocol.

Pulsar Ecosystem

Creating Pulsar and making it an open source project provided the building blocks for sound and flexible messaging. Since then, developers have built powerful tools to couple with Pulsar's underlying technology. In addition to the three projects highlighted in this section, the Pulsar community is active with thousands of users in Slack channels and messaging boards.

Pulsar Functions

At its core, Pulsar is about performant messaging and storage. We've talked at length in this chapter about Pulsar's flexible design for data storage and scalability. Pulsar Functions answer the question of how to process data stored within Pulsar. They are lightweight compute processes that can consume data from a Pulsar topic, perform some computation, and then publish the results to another Pulsar topic.

Pulsar Functions draw inspiration from Functions as a Service implementations such as Google Cloud Functions and Amazon Web Services Lambda Functions. Specifically, Pulsar Functions have a flexible deployment model in which resources can be coupled with Pulsar broker nodes or run as a separate process. Pulsar Functions both receive and output to Pulsar topics (see Figure 3-9).

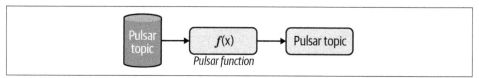

Figure 3-9. This Pulsar function is receiving a topic, performing some processing, and sending it to another topic.

Pulsar Functions align well with the design principle of modularity. Though Pulsar's core is written in Java, you can write Pulsar Functions in Java, Python, or Go. The choice to separate Pulsar's runtime from Pulsar Functions' runtime reduces the learning curve for programmers who want to learn Pulsar and interact with it. Pulsar Functions are an optional way to process messages in Pulsar. If a user wants to continue using their current stream processing framework, they can do that instead. Pulsar Functions also provide a high-quality stream processing implementation that has a shallow learning curve; if you can write in Java, Python, or Go, you can write semantically correct stream processing without learning a new framework.

Pulsar IO

Pulsar IO is a connector framework for Pulsar that allows Pulsar topics to become input or output for other processes. To understand Pulsar IO, it's a bit more instructive to think of an end-to-end example. Suppose you want to create a pipeline that reads in data from your MySQL database row by row and then stores it in an Elasticsearch index. (*Elasticsearch* is an open source search engine technology. An *index* is a named entity in Elasticsearch by which the documents are organized. You can think of them as analogous to a database in relational database parlance.) Pulsar IO can facilitate this entire application with just configuration (see Figure 3-10).

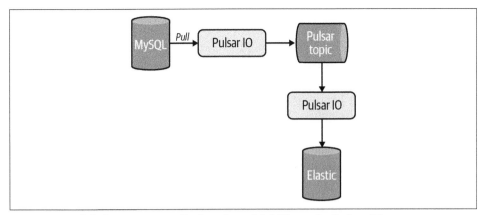

Figure 3-10. A Pulsar process pulls data from MySQL, and a Pulsar IO process moves data from the Pulsar topic to Elasticsearch.

Like Pulsar Functions, Pulsar IO provides an isolated and scalable compute process to facilitate the event-driven movement of data through Pulsar topics to destinations. In Pulsar Functions, the interface is a Pulsar topic; in Pulsar IO, the interface can be a Pulsar topic or an external system. Pulsar IO has some philosophical and implementation similarities to Kafka Connect. Like Kafka Connect, Pulsar IO is designed to enable ease of use for everyday use cases with Pulsar. I'll go into considerably more detail and give examples of using Pulsar IO and building our application in Chapter 7.

Pulsar SQL

Pulsar's decoupled compute and storage architecture allows it to store more data for more extended periods. With all of the data stored in Pulsar, querying data on Pulsar is a natural next step. Pulsar SQL provides a scalable compute runtime that enables SQL queries to be executed against Pulsar topics. Pulsar SQL uses Apache Presto, a SQL-on-Anything engine, to provide the compute resources to query Pulsar topics.

Pulsar SQL has some philosophical similarities to Kafka's KSQL. Both are designed to allow the querying of topics with SQL syntax. Pulsar SQL is a read-only system designed to query topics and not necessarily create permanent data views. KSQL, on the other hand, is interactive and allows users to create new topics based on the results of SQL queries. You'll learn more about Pulsar SQL implementation and use cases in Chapter 10.

Pulsar Success Stories

So far in this chapter, we've talked at length about how and why Apache Pulsar was developed, the Pulsar ecosystem, and the unique challenges that resulted when Pulsar became an open source system. Can Pulsar address the problems of companies today? Does a platform like Pulsar created in the private cloud of Yahoo! work for companies hosted on the public cloud? These are essential questions for teams that are evaluating Pulsar for their messaging needs. In this section, we'll cover three companies that adopted Pulsar and have been successful with it. These stories highlight a business problem that engineering teams turned to Pulsar to explain, and they describe how Pulsar helped them solve the problem.

Yahoo! JAPAN

In 2017, Yahoo! JAPAN managed about 70 billion page views per month. At the time, it faced challenges around managing the load on its servers and orchestrating hundreds of services in its service-oriented architecture. Along with the challenges of running its services at scale, Yahoo! JAPAN wished to distribute its entire architecture across countries (geo-replication). Yahoo! JAPAN looked to a messaging system to help with each of these problems. The company investigated Apache Pulsar and Apache Kafka for its workflow needs and reported the results of the investigation in a blog post published in 2019 (*https://oreil.ly/8K6Hw*).

The authors of the post detail some of the key differences between Pulsar and Kafka and why they ultimately chose Pulsar for their workloads. The three most important features that influenced their choice were the following:

- Geo-replication
- Reliability
- Flexibility

While Pulsar and Kafka scored similarly on reliability, Pulsar took a commanding lead in terms of geo-replication and flexibility. At the time of their investigation, little had been published on cross-datacenter deployments of Kafka. Meanwhile, the Pulsar story around geo-replication was well known in the community (as stated in this chapter's opening). Ultimately, Yahoo! JAPAN chose Pulsar and has used it for many years to power its services. Pulsar provides the engine for its service-oriented architecture and removes many of the burdens that come with geo-replication.

Splunk

Splunk is a corporation that makes the collection, aggregation, and searching of logs and other telemetry data easy (see Figure 3-11). Hundreds of enterprise technology companies use Splunk to collect logs from their applications, instrument their applications, and troubleshoot their infrastructure and applications. In 2019, Splunk acquired Streamlio, the first managed offering of Apache Pulsar. In the press release announcing the acquisition (*https://oreil.ly/o98lq*), Splunk notes that Apache Pulsar is a unique technology and that it will be transformative for the company. It's not hard for a company like Splunk to imagine how technology like Pulsar is used in its products. In a 2020 talk titled "How Splunk Mission Control Leverages Various Pulsar Subscription Types" (*https://oreil.ly/PPQ77*), Pranav Dharma, then a senior software engineer at Splunk, covers how Splunk uses Pulsar's flexible subscription model to power its center of operations. The flexible subscription allows the company to provide a range of message processing guarantees based on application needs. We'll talk about subscriptions in more detail in Chapter 6.

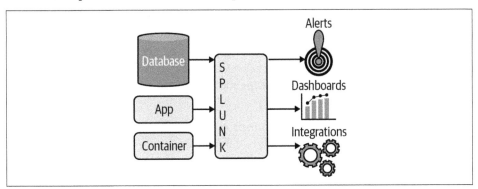

Figure 3-11. Applications and databases forward their logs and metrics to Splunk, and Splunk indexes them and makes them searchable.

In another 2020 talk titled "Why Splunk Chose Pulsar" (*https://oreil.ly/LA1DA*), Karthik Ramasamy, distinguished engineer at Splunk and founder of Streamlio, details the wins that Splunk gets from Pulsar geo-replication, low-latency message transmission, and scalable storage via Apache BookKeeper. Pulsar was a significant investment for Splunk, but by all accounts, it was a worthwhile one. Splunk leverages Pulsar's core performance to make quick decisions and its flexible subscription model to provide a single platform to handle all messaging needs.

Iterable

Iterable is a customer engagement platform designed to make customer lifecycle marketing, recommendation systems, and cross-channel engagement easy. To scale its operations across thousands of customers, Iterable needed a messaging platform that could be the foundation of its software interactions. Initially, Iterable used RabbitMQ, but the company ran into the system's limitations and turned to other systems to solve its messaging problems. In an article titled "How Apache Pulsar Is Helping Iterable Scale Its Customer Engagement Platform" (*https://oreil.ly/7bg34*), author Greg Methvin lays out the problems Iterable looked to solve with a new messaging platform. The three key features he and his team looked for were:

Scalability
Iterable needed a system that would scale up to the demand of its users.

Reliability
Iterable needed a system that could reliably store its messaging data.

Flexibility
Iterable needed a system that would handle all of its messaging needs.

Iterable evaluated several messaging platforms, including Apache Kafka, Amazon's Simple Queue Service (SQS), and Kinesis. In the evaluation, Pulsar was the only system that provided the required semantics and scalability. Iterable used its messaging platform for both queuing and streaming. While Kinesis and Kafka provided some facilities for accomplishing this, they fell short of Pulsar's elegance and general-purpose mechanism. Additionally, Pulsar's decoupled architecture provided the flexibility Iterable needed to scale topics independently, as well as the proper semantics in terms of topics.

By choosing Pulsar as the event backbone of its architecture, Iterable has been able to scale and meet new and growing customer demands.

Summary

In this chapter, we focused exclusively on the use cases for Apache Pulsar, and specifically on some large companies that have used (and continue to use) Pulsar as a cornerstone technology. You learned that Pulsar is especially suitable for the following:

- Low-latency messaging requirements
- Geo-replication
- Problems that require queueing and event streams

We covered the need for streaming technology in Chapter 1, we discussed the publish/subscribe method in Chapter 2, and now we have some sufficient motivation for the uniqueness of Pulsar and are prepared to unpack its pieces in Chapter 4.

Pulsar Internals

So far, we've discussed the motivation for using a system like Apache Pulsar, the historical context in which Pulsar was created, and some companies that use Pulsar to power their systems. Now we have sufficient context to pull the covers from Pulsar and explore the components and, more important, why they work together. We'll start by looking at each of Pulsar's components (see Figure 4-1): namely Pulsar brokers, Apache BookKeeper, and Apache ZooKeeper. Then we'll take a look at a standard technology used across all three of these projects: the Java programming language and the Java virtual machine.

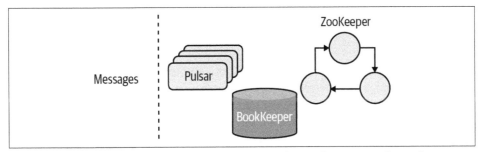

Figure 4-1. Pulsar's components include nodes, Apache BookKeeper, and Apache ZooKeeper.

Brokers

As noted earlier, Pulsar's modularity allows the system to separate its responsibilities and select the best technology to handle each one. One of Pulsar's responsibilities is to provide an interface so that publishers and subscribers can connect to it.

Pulsar brokers handle this as well as the following tasks (see Figure 4-2):

- Temporary management of topic data storage
- Communication with Apache BookKeeper and ZooKeeper
- Schema validation
- Inter-broker communication
- Runtime environments for Pulsar Functions and Pulsar IO

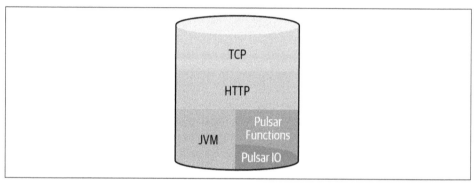

Figure 4-2. Pulsar nodes have an underlying implementation in Java on the Java virtual machine. Pulsar Functions and Pulsar IO are also implemented in Java. Pulsar supports several HTTP and TCP points for communication within the cluster.

Let's take a closer look at Pulsar brokers.

Message Cache

Pulsar brokers are stateless, in that they do not store any data on the Pulsar broker disks that are used in the message lifecycle. Pulsar is unique among message brokers in this approach, as most similar systems couple the storage and retrieval of messages in some way. Being stateless has advantages as well as disadvantages. The disadvantages are that another system is required to take on state management and some abstractions are required to translate from Pulsar's storage needs to the storage system. The advantages are that storage requirements are separate from compute requirements and that a more fault-tolerant storage layer results.

If Pulsar brokers were responsible for storing the state of topics on the broker, a number of questions would arise regarding how to store data on the brokers and how to handle failure scenarios.

Since we're just beginning our journey with Pulsar, let's keep it simple and explore just the following three considerations:

- Storing data
- Adding new nodes to the cluster
- Removing nodes from the cluster

In Chapter 3, we discussed what storing data in a distributed system looks like in terms of storage and retrieval for a low-volume system. A high-volume system has even more things to consider when it comes to how data is distributed across nodes and how events like losing a node impact the entire system. Instead of taking on the complexity of understanding the storage problem, Pulsar chose to rely on Apache BookKeeper for storage and to use the brokers as stateless orchestrators of the storage.

Pulsar uses an abstraction on top of BookKeeper, called a managed ledger. The managed ledger works as a bridge between the messages that Pulsar brokers need to store and the ledgers in BookKeeper (covered later in this chapter). You can think of ledgers as the highest storage abstraction in BookKeeper. The managed ledger is an API that keeps track of the ledger sizes and states and when it's time to start a new ledger.

Figure 4-3 shows a typical topology of a Pulsar topic. Broker 1 is responsible for topic reads and writes. For reads, it writes to all the BookKeeper instances (main servers, or bookies) that are part of the ensemble for the topic; for reads, it requests data from the leader for that ledger. The managed ledger manages that interface. Does this mean that for every write Pulsar broker has to retrieve data from the bookies? Not exactly. Pulsar brokers have a managed ledger cache that allows some messages to be cached on the broker for a consumer.

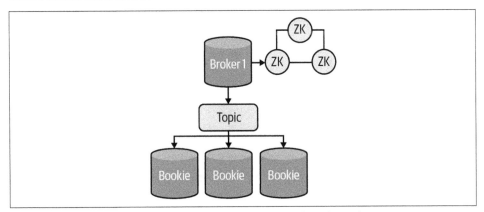

Figure 4-3. In this Apache Pulsar cluster, bookies store data from the topic.

In a streaming context, each message needs to be written to BookKeeper. Instead of writing to BookKeeper and reading from it for an active consumer, Pulsar brokers can simply tail the latest events directly to an active consumer. This avoids making round trips to BookKeeper, as depicted in Figure 4-4.

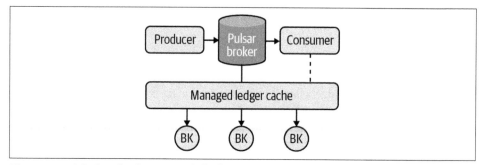

Figure 4-4. A Pulsar broker can tail the latest events directly to an active consumer.

It's important to remember that even though the managed ledger can cache values for consumers that are subscribed to the topic, the cache is only a cache (see Figure 4-5). Caches are ephemeral and are created and destroyed easily. They are not supposed to be permanent data stores, as data that is stored in a cache is a convenience but also a potential headache. Fortunately, Pulsar brokers have a limited scope in which they cache data. In Chapters 5 and 6 you'll learn more about Pulsar's messaging lifecycle.

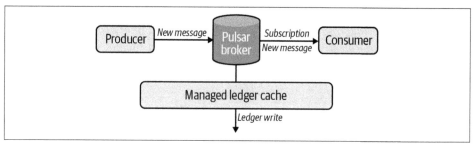

Figure 4-5. The managed ledger cache is a configurable cache kept by the Pulsar broker. It stores a ledger of data stored in BookKeeper and keeps an interface to write to BookKeeper.

BookKeeper and ZooKeeper Communication

As discussed in this chapter's introduction, Pulsar nodes work in conjunction with BookKeeper and ZooKeeper as the messaging platform's backbone. Not surprisingly, Pulsar brokers need to communicate with ZooKeeper and BookKeeper for topic management and other configuration values. How and when this communication takes place is fully managed by the Pulsar brokers. It's worth taking some time to better understand when brokers communicate with BookKeeper and ZooKeeper.

ZooKeeper stores all metadata related to the Pulsar cluster. This includes metadata about which broker is the leader for a topic, configuration values for service discovery, and other administrative data. Much of the data stored in ZooKeeper is cached on the Pulsar nodes, and there is a configuration-driven lifecycle about when to pull new data from ZooKeeper. Communicating with ZooKeeper is a constant part of Pulsar's lifecycle.

As discussed in previous sections, BookKeeper is the storage engine in Pulsar. All message data is stored in Pulsar. Every message stored and retrieved from Pulsar requires communication with BookKeeper. BookKeeper's communication interfaces are covered in more detail in Chapter 12.

Schema Validation

Schema validation is the process of ensuring that new messages published to a Pulsar topic adhere to a predefined shape. To ensure that a message adheres to a schema, Pulsar brokers work with the Pulsar schema registry to perform that validation. The lifecycle of schema validation is covered in Chapter 6; however, the responsibility of ensuring schema is significant and falls squarely on the brokers, so we'll discuss it briefly here.

Brokers handle schema validation in two key ways. First, they are the point of ownership for schemas as they relate to topics. Brokers answer the following questions:

- Does this topic have a schema associated with it?
- What is the schema associated with the topic?
- Does this schema require that new messages adhere to the schema?

Also, brokers can ensure validation of in-flight messages. Schema validation is an important part of end-to-end messaging systems, and Pulsar brokers serve this purpose, among others.

Inter-Broker Communication

As mentioned previously, brokers are responsible for the reads and writes of specific topics. It is possible for a client to request data from a broker that is not responsible for that topic. What happens in this case? Figure 4-6 depicts this. Each broker uses metadata stored in ZooKeeper to determine whether it is the leader (the one responsible for the topic) and, if it is not the leader, who the leader is. The broker may route the client to the correct broker to start publishing (or retrieving) messages.

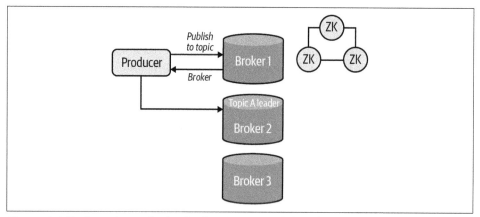

Figure 4-6. Broker 1 is not the leader for Topic A and therefore redirects the producers to the correct topic.

Pulsar Functions and Pulsar IO

At the beginning of this section, I stressed the importance of modularity in Pulsar's design. In the sections that followed, you learned how much responsibility falls on the brokers. It may have occurred to you that perhaps Pulsar's design could be more modular. It's important to remember two things when considering modularity. First, does it make sense to remove the responsibilities from the brokers and put them elsewhere? And second, would moving those responsibilities elsewhere necessarily improve Pulsar as far as reliability and scalability are concerned? As a general rule, the answer to both questions is no. The exceptions to this rule are Pulsar IO and Pulsar Functions.

Pulsar as a project provides some easy methods for getting started with the base Pulsar brokers as well as extensions such as Pulsar Functions and Pulsar IO. You can use Pulsar Functions or Pulsar IO for a new Pulsar user without additional overhead or difficulty. The limiting factor to this convenience is that brokers are the primary source for throughput in Pulsar. How many messages a cluster can ingest per second is highly influenced by a broker's availability. If the broker is busy processing Pulsar Functions or Pulsar IO tasks, it will impact the entire system's performance.

In many cases this performance degradation won't be problematic, but for sufficient scale, moving your Pulsar IO or Pulsar function to another cluster would be an improvement. Fortunately, Pulsar provides a mechanism for precisely this.

Apache BookKeeper

Apache BookKeeper (*https://oreil.ly/dOm7v*) is a general-purpose data storage system. BookKeeper, like Pulsar and ZooKeeper, was developed at Yahoo! in the 2010s to meet the following requirements:

- Write and read latencies of < 5 ms
- Durable, consistent, and fault-tolerant data storage
- Read data as it is written
- Provide an interface for real-time and long-term storage

BookKeeper is an ambitious project, aimed at building primitives for storage that could work for a wide number of projects and long into the future. BookKeeper is written in Java and heavily utilizes Apache ZooKeeper (which we'll cover later in this chapter). Figure 4-7 shows BookKeeper's architecture. The main servers are called bookies, and they can be arranged as a cluster (ZooKeeper can be arranged in the same way). The bookies contain an underlying storage system called a ledger.

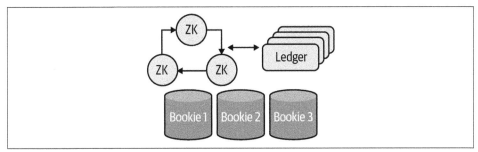

Figure 4-7. Bookies are servers where data is stored (on a ledger). Apache ZooKeeper (ZK) manages service discovery and coordination among the bookies.

How do you go about building a system with the performance requirements and durability promised by Apache BookKeeper? The breakdown of requirements from a high level is as follows:

- A simple semantic for storing data
- A fault-tolerant way to distribute the storage of data across nodes
- An easy way to recover from any individual node failure

Starting with the first requirement, Apache BookKeeper implements an append-only log called a *ledger*. A ledger consists of arbitrary data called *entries*. A sequence of ledgers is called a *stream* (see Figure 4-8).

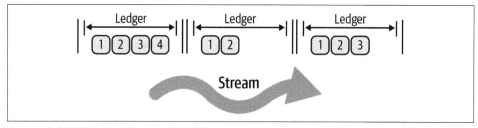

Figure 4-8. A high-level view of BookKeeper storage. The stream is a collection of ledgers, and ledgers are composed of smaller entries.

Creating entries and ledgers with the Apache BookKeeper Java client is simple as well. BookKeeper has two Java APIs: the BookKeeper Ledger API and the Advanced Ledger API. The BookKeeper Ledger API is lower level, focused on allowing the user to interact directly with ledgers. The Advanced Ledger API provides some additional features that give the user more fine-grained control around quorum configuration (covered shortly) and other aspects of transaction safety for BookKeeper. For our purposes, we'll do a few things with the Ledger API to illustrate what it might look like to interact with BookKeeper directly.

We'll perform these operations:

- Create a new BookKeeper client
- Create a ledger
- Write entries to the ledger
- Close the ledger
- Reopen the ledger
- Read all entries

To begin, take a look at the following code:

```
// Create a client object for the local ensemble.
BookKeeper bkc = new BookKeeper("localhost:2181");

// A password for the new ledger
byte[] ledgerPassword = /* a sequence of bytes */;

// Create a new ledger and get identifier
LedgerHandle lh = bkc.createLedger(BookKeeper.DigestType.MAC, ledgerPassword);
long ledgerId = lh.getId();

// Create a buffer for ten-byte entries
ByteBuffer entry = ByteBuffer.allocate(10);

int numberOfEntries = 100;
```

```
// Add entries to the ledger, then close the ledger
for (int i = 0; i < numberOfEntries; i++){
      entry.putInt(i);
      entry.position(0);
      lh.addEntry(entry.array());
}
lh.close();

// Reopen the ledger
lh = bkc.openLedger(ledgerId, BookKeeper.DigestType.MAC, ledgerPassword);

// Read all entries
Enumeration<LedgerEntry> entries = lh.readEntries(0, numberOfEntries - 1);

while(entries.hasMoreElements()) {
      ByteBuffer result = ByteBuffer.wrap(ls.nextElement().getEntry());
      Integer retrEntry = result.getInt();

    // Get all entries printed
    System.out.println(String.format("Result: %s", retrEntry));
}

// Close the ledger and stop the client
lh.close();
bkc.close();
```

The preceding code gives us significant context to move on to the second question we laid out, which is how do we store segments across multiple nodes?

Apache BookKeeper uses quorum-based replication to manage the problem of distributing data across nodes. The protocol has some complexities, but we can focus on the main aspect of it to better understand how it relates to Pulsar topics.

The BookKeeper protocol requires the following for every ledger:

The ensemble size (E)
    Represents the number of bookies the ledger will be stored on.

The quorum write size (Q_w)
    Represents the number of nodes each entry will be written to.

The quorum acknowledgment (ack) size (Q_a)
    Represents the number of nodes an entry must be acknowledged by.

In general, the ensemble has to be greater than or equal to the quorum write size. This is a sensible requirement because you can't have more bookies that accept a new ledger than there are in the entire cluster. Also, the quorum ack size must be less than or equal to the quorum write size. This also makes sense because, at a minimum, you want every write node to acknowledge the write of a new entry, but reducing the number of nodes required to acknowledge new entries might increase overall performance without having any impact on the redundancy or safety of the data.[1]

It may be helpful to walk through a few examples. Figure 4-9 depicts a BookKeeper configuration in which the ensemble size is 3, the quorum write size is 3, and the quorum ack size is 3. Each new ledger is written to every bookie and every bookie must acknowledge their writing.

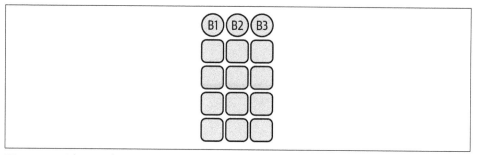

Figure 4-9. This BookKeeper quorum has four ledgers (represented as squares) and an ensemble size of 3, a quorum write size of 3, and a quorum ack size of 3.

Figure 4-10 depicts an ensemble of 5, with a quorum write size of 3 and a quorum ack size of 3. In this scenario, each ledger is written to only three bookies.

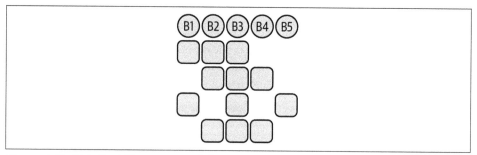

Figure 4-10. This BookKeeper example has an ensemble of 5, with a quorum write size of 3 and a quorum ack size of 3.

Now that you know a bit about BookKeeper's storage internals, let's take a step back and examine some of the new terminology and ideas I just introduced.

Quorums are used a lot in organizational contexts, but in distributed system contexts, a quorum is simply a group of processes. For BookKeeper, quorums are used for ledger management, but they are also used as a mechanism for keeping track of

---

1 If you have a significantly large write size, then even if one node fails to receive a write the data is replicated by enough nodes for a recovery in the event of a node failure.

which bookies are the leaders for a given segment. We won't get into the topic of leader election here, but Figure 4-11 provides a decent high-level overview of the concept.

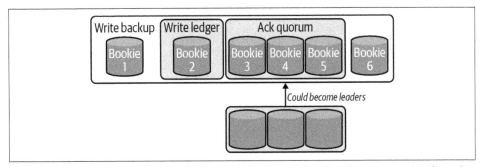

Figure 4-11. Leader election in BookKeeper. Bookies are leaders for segments and can be removed or changed by a new leader election event.

Now that you understand the basics of storage, you'll notice that BookKeeper provides the basic building blocks for storing data and keeping it safe. A single bookie may contain a fragment of a ledger, and that fragment is replicated across several bookies. Figure 4-12 shows what this might look like for three ledgers across three bookies.

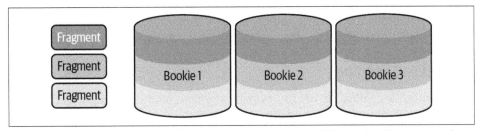

Figure 4-12. Fragments (parts of ledgers) are stored across different bookies in a Book-Keeper ensemble.

The design and storage primitives in BookKeeper make it suitable for complex ledgers that can span an ever-increasing number of bookies, as depicted in Figure 4-13.

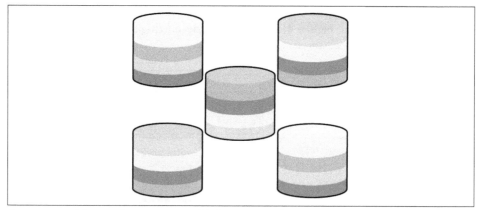

Figure 4-13. This BookKeeper ensemble has several fragments spanning bookies.

You may be wondering how this system benefits Apache Pulsar. Topics (the fundamental message storage paradigm in Pulsar) are implemented on BookKeeper. In a system where every message is critical, BookKeeper makes it virtually impossible[2] to lose any messages. Additionally, BookKeeper ledgers are an append-only log. As such, it's the perfect primitive for storing data for an event streaming system, as discussed in Chapter 2.

There is a lot more to BookKeeper (*https://oreil.ly/JgpTL*), but hopefully this section provided some insight into its elegance. Storage of Pulsar messages is one use case for BookKeeper; let's explore a few others to solidify our understanding.

Write-Ahead Logging

A write-ahead log (WAL) is used to provide atomicity and durability in a database system. This book isn't about databases, but the WAL is a critical concept to understand in order to grasp the value of BookKeeper. If you think about a database table, you can perform actions such as inserts, updates, selects, and deletes. When you perform an insert, update, or delete, the database writes your desire to perform that action to a log (see Figure 4-14). The database can then check against the log to validate it performed the action intended by the user. WALs are not only useful for ensuring guarantees in databases; they are also used for change data capture (CDC). Pulsar IO utilizes WALs in databases to perform CDC (we'll cover this in Chapter 7).

---

2 A poorly configured cluster can lose data.

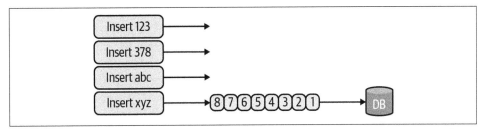

Figure 4-14. In this write-ahead log implementation, each new event is written to a log before it is executed on the underlying database storage engine.

BookKeeper's durability properties, fault tolerance, and scalability make it the right choice for a WAL implementation. Additionally, BookKeeper can scale separately from the database if needed, providing modularity and loose coupling.

Message Storing

Every messaging system has some implementation for storing messages temporarily. A message broker's value is in the reliable transport of messages, after all. How we implement that storage will have some downstream consequences on how the data can be used later. For systems like Pulsar, Kafka, and Pravega, message durability is paramount. BookKeeper's model of ledger storage is the perfect abstraction for storing an event stream (see Figure 4-15).

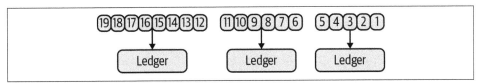

Figure 4-15. This topic has sequential data written to BookKeeper ledgers.

Following are some of the properties that make BookKeeper a good solution for event stream data:

- Append-only logging
- Highly durable
- Easily distributed

Object/Blob Storage

Object stores allow the storage of arbitrarily large objects for future retrieval. Systems like Amazon S3, Google Cloud Storage, and Azure Blob Storage are popular because they offer a simple API to store and retrieve items from the cloud. In cloud systems, object storage is used for storing images, arbitrary files on behalf of users, and large data lakes. Implementing an object store requires elasticity, or the ability to add new nodes to the cluster without disrupting ongoing operations. It also requires fault tolerance; if nodes in the cluster fail, there should be a reliable backup in the cluster somewhere. In addition, it requires the ability to store and retrieve objects of all kinds. Apache BookKeeper can perform all these tasks and can perform them well. BlobIt is an object store built on top of BookKeeper. It allows for the storage of arbitrarily large objects, and all of the storage is managed with BookKeeper. A user can send a CSV file to BlobIt and the file will be stored on BookKeeper as depicted in Figure 4-16.

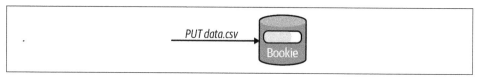

Figure 4-16. You can store a CSV file on BookKeeper for use as a general-purpose object store.

While BookKeeper can store arbitrarily large data, the complexity in using it as an object store is in managing the movement of the data to and from bytes. BlobIt relies on the distributed and fault-tolerant nature of BookKeeper, and adds value by making an Amazon S3–compliant API.

Pravega

Pravega is a distributed messaging system that has a lot of similarities to Pulsar. Developed at Dell, Pravega builds on the concept of a stream as the fundamental building block for storage. Pravega uses BookKeeper in a similar way to Pulsar (see Figure 4-17): storing all topic and cursor data. Like Pulsar, BookKeeper enables Pravega to scale storage and message throughput independently, and it provides durability for and fault tolerance within a Pravega cluster.

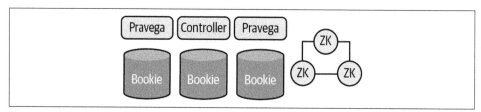

Figure 4-17. Pravega architecture. Similar to Apache Pulsar, Pravega uses BookKeeper for long-term storage, uses ZooKeeper for distributed coordination, and has some responsibilities that are owned by the Pravega servers.

An additional interesting tidbit about Pravega is that its use cases extend beyond just event streaming data (an area that Pulsar is focused on). Pravega is also suitable for streaming video data and large files. As mentioned previously, you can store any data on BookKeeper; the challenges lie in how that data is presented and how end users interact with it.

Majordodo

Majordodo is a resource manager that handles the scheduling of bespoke workloads on ephemeral clusters. Majordodo tracks the resources used in a cluster, the available resources in a cluster, and other metadata about jobs running in a cluster (see Figure 4-18). Majordodo (*https://oreil.ly/kh1T4*) utilizes BookKeeper ledgers to track the starting, running, and completion of jobs on the cluster. Since BookKeeper provides low read and write latencies, scheduling workloads is a novel but worthy use. Majordodo is developed and maintained by Diennea, a technology company that helps build scalable digital brand solutions.

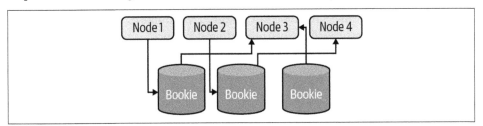

Figure 4-18. A Majordodo cluster. BookKeeper manages data storage for each node so that any node in the cluster can pick up work or distribute existing work.

In the preceding sections, we spent a lot of time talking about the importance and use cases for BookKeeper. ZooKeeper works in conjunction with BookKeeper and plays a different but equally important role in Pulsar and in the wider software ecosystem. ZooKeeper is discussed in the next section.

Apache ZooKeeper

Apache ZooKeeper was developed at Yahoo! in the late 2000s, and the Apache Software Foundation made it an open source platform in 2011. ZooKeeper implements the system described in the 2006 paper "The Chubby Lock Service for Loosely-Coupled Distributed Systems" by Mike Burrows,[3] a distinguished engineer at Google.

---

3 Mike Burrows, "Chubby lock service for loosely-coupled distributed systems," *OSDI '06: Proceedings of the 7th Symposium on Operating Systems Design and Implementation* (November 2006): 24.

The paper explains why Google needed Chubby to manage its sprawling internal systems and provides some high-level descriptions of its implementation.

Chubby provides tools for distributed configuration management, service discovery, and a two-phase commit implementation. Chubby is a proprietary service used within Google, and the paper provides a peek at how Google handled a standard set of distributed system problems. With some light shed on how to approach these problems, Yahoo! implemented Apache ZooKeeper.

ZooKeeper provides an open source implementation suitable for coordinating distributed systems. ZooKeeper's primary requirements are:

- Performance
- Fault tolerance
- Reliability

By meeting these requirements, ZooKeeper is suitable for implementing several distributed system algorithms, including Paxos and Raft. Another standard implementation on top of ZooKeeper is the two-phase commit protocol. The two-phase commit ensures atomicity, or that all nodes have a shared understanding of the system's current state in a distributed system. The two-phase commit is illustrated in Figure 4-19.

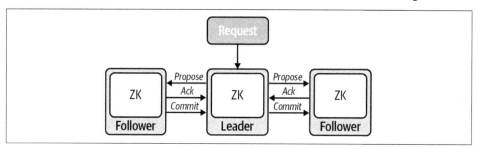

Figure 4-19. In this two-phase commit, a new change is accepted by the leader and immediately sent to followers as part of a single transaction.

In Pulsar, ZooKeeper manages the BookKeeper configuration and distributed consensus, and stores metadata about Pulsar topics and configuration. It plays an integral role in all Pulsar operations, and replacing it would be difficult. It's worth diving into a few examples of use cases for ZooKeeper to understand its importance to Pulsar.

Naming Service

One common way systems integrate with Apache ZooKeeper is as a naming service. A naming service maps network resources to their respective addresses. In a system with many nodes, keeping track of their identity and their place in the network can be tricky. Apache Mesos uses ZooKeeper for this purpose (among others). In a Mesos cluster, ZooKeeper stores every node, their status, and a leader or follower. If nodes need to coordinate, ZooKeeper can be used as a lookup. ZooKeeper serves this purpose in Apache Pulsar as well, as depicted in Figure 4-6 earlier in this chapter.

Configuration Management

Apache Pulsar has about 150 configuration values that are tunable by Pulsar operators. Each value changes the underlying behavior of Pulsar, ZooKeeper, or BookKeeper. Some of those configurations impact the publishing and consumption of messages in the Pulsar cluster. Pulsar brokers store their configuration in ZooKeeper because a reliable and highly available place to retrieve and store those configurations is paramount.

In some ways, ZooKeeper is a safe, distributed storage engine. As Figure 4-20 shows, ZooKeeper can keep track of named keys and values.

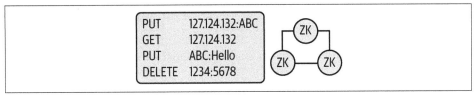

Figure 4-20. A ZooKeeper cluster can store multiple configuration values.

Leader Election

Leader election is the process of choosing a leader for a specific set of responsibilities in a distributed system. In Apache Pulsar, a broker is the leader of a topic (or one or more partitions in a partitioned topic). If that broker goes offline, a new broker is elected the leader of that same topic or partition(s). Building on both the naming service use case and the configuration use case, ZooKeeper can provide a reliable building block for implementing leader election. It keeps track of leaders, knows where they are in the cluster, and can be called on to implement new leaders in the future, as depicted in Figure 4-21.

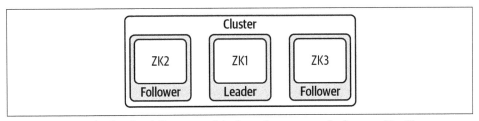

Figure 4-21. In this leader-follower model, the values are tracked across ZooKeeper nodes.

Notification System

The final ZooKeeper use case that we'll cover is that of a notification system. In Chapter 1, you learned how notifications can help patients in a hospital receive better care. The most important aspects of a notification system are the timely delivery of notifications and the guaranteed delivery of notifications. If you miss a notification about engagement on a tweet you sent late last night, that isn't a world-stopping event. However, if you miss a notification to renew your driver's license, you may be arrested the next time you are pulled over. We've discussed how ZooKeeper serves as a high-quality naming service. The same qualities that make ZooKeeper a good naming service make it an excellent notification system. Namely, we can ensure that the system state is shared by all parties, and that if a party doesn't have that notification, we can quickly determine it using ZooKeeper. Figure 4-22 provides a high-level view of this concept.

Figure 4-22. The commit protocol used in ZooKeeper is useful as a notification protocol.

Apache Kafka

Apache Kafka is a distributed messaging system suitable for event streaming. It has broad adoption because of its thoughtful API design and scalability characteristics. Developed at LinkedIn and made freely available in 2014, Kafka provides the building blocks for event management and real-time systems at companies around the world. As of version 2.5, Kafka utilizes Apache ZooKeeper for configuration management and leader election. ZooKeeper plays a critical role in fault tolerance and message delivery in a Kafka cluster. Figure 4-23 depicts a Kafka cluster with Apache ZooKeeper.

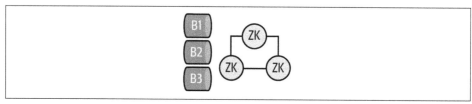

Figure 4-23. This Apache Kafka cluster has three brokers, as well as ZooKeeper for coordination and leader election.

Interestingly, the Kafka project removed the requirement of ZooKeeper in a Kafka cluster as of version 2.8 and replaced the ZooKeeper responsibilities with a Raft consensus implementation within the cluster itself. Figure 4-24 depicts this change.

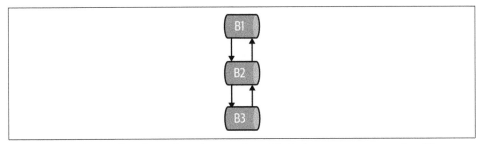

Figure 4-24. This Kafka cluster has three nodes with their own consensus algorithm, known as KRaft (Kafka Raft).

Apache Druid

Apache Druid is a real-time analytics database originally developed by Metamarkets in 2011 and made freely available through the Apache Software Foundation in 2015. Druid powers the analytics suite of companies like Alibaba, Airbnb, and Booking.com. Unlike SQL-on-Anything engines[4] such as Presto and Apache Spark, Druid stores and indexes data and queries it. As a distributed system, Druid uses ZooKeeper for configuration management and consensus management (see Figure 4-25). ZooKeeper plays a critical role in allowing Druid clusters to scale out without management overhead or performance degradation.

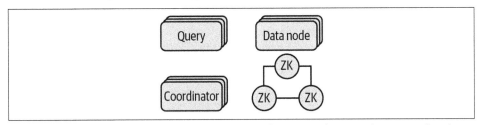

Figure 4-25. This Apache Druid cluster consists of query nodes, coordinator nodes, data storage nodes, and ZooKeeper for configuration management and service discovery.

Pulsar Proxy

While Pulsar brokers are the communication mechanism for Pulsar clients, in cases when the brokers are deployed in a private network scenario, we may need a way to expose communication with the outside world. Figure 4-26 shows an example of such a scenario.

---

4 SQL-on-Anything is a query engine that enables users to write SQL queries against files, representational state transfer (REST). APIs, databases, and other sources of data. We will cover this topic in more detail in Chapter 10.

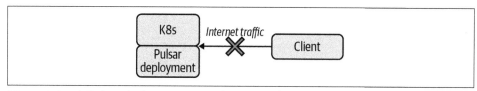

Figure 4-26. A Pulsar deployment on Kubernetes. The client tries to reach Pulsar over the internet, but the brokers cannot be exposed and Pulsar cannot be reached.

A Pulsar proxy is an optional gateway that simplifies the process of exposing brokers to outside traffic. A proxy can be deployed as an additional service and serve the role of taking on internet traffic and routing the messages to the right broker (see Figure 4-27).

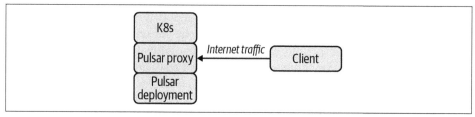

Figure 4-27. This Pulsar proxy is exposing brokers on the Kubernetes deployment to the internet so that a client can reach it.

In many cases, we should have an additional load-balancing layer, called a proxy frontend, to handle the concerns of edge internet traffic (see Figure 4-28).

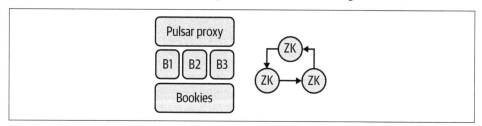

Figure 4-28. In this configuration, the proxy handles all internet traffic. However, it is better suited for routing traffic across brokers.

Proxy frontends such as HAProxy and NGINX are purpose built for handling internet scale traffic. Using these with a Pulsar proxy as a destination can help ease the load on the proxy (see Figure 4-29).

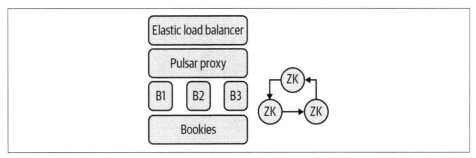

Figure 4-29. A load balancer in front of a Pulsar proxy. In this scenario, the load balancer manages communication with clients and the proxy works more as a forwarder.

The common thread between ZooKeeper, BookKeeper, and Pulsar is the Java programming language and the Java virtual machine (JVM). Let's turn our attention to the JVM and the role it plays in Pulsar projects.

Java Virtual Machine (JVM)

Pulsar brokers, Apache BookKeeper, and Apache ZooKeeper are written in the Java programming language and run on the Java virtual machine (JVM). Earlier in this chapter, we explored a Pulsar broker's components and noted that a broker is primarily an HTTP server that implements a special TCP protocol (depicted in Figure 4-30). Nothing within Pulsar screams that it should have been written in Java, so why was Java chosen for Pulsar years ago, and is it still a good choice today?

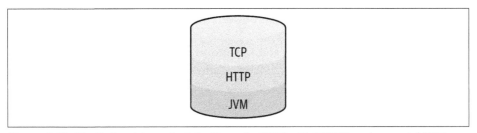

Figure 4-30. The Pulsar hierarchy is built on the JVM with HTTP and a special TCP protocol.

To understand why Yahoo! chose Java, it's essential to consider the environment in which Pulsar was born. Pulsar's creation dates back to 2013 (*https://oreil.ly/pXKjo*), when Yahoo! experienced unparalleled user growth. As Yahoo! grew, it ran into unprecedented challenges in the storage, transmission, and retrieval of data. At the time, the Hadoop ecosystem powered the storage and retrieval systems for most web-scale companies. With Hadoop, many of the tools used to build distributed consensus and configuration management were born and written in Java. Apache Mesos (see Figure 4-31) was one of these systems.

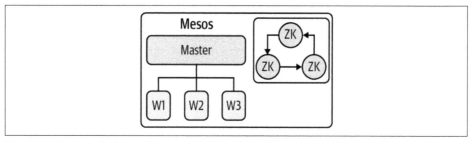

Figure 4-31. Apache Mesos is a container orchestration engine that is written in Java and utilizes Apache ZooKeeper.[5]

The first and most pragmatic reason to choose Java and the JVM is that many developers know the Java programming language. According to Slashdot, the number of Java developers as of 2018 was 7.3 million. That is a significant percentage of the overall total of 23 million developers. As an open source project, Pulsar can have a lot more success by tapping into a more extensive developer market.

In addition, the Java ecosystem is vast. There are Java libraries for just about everything, and when implementing a platform for all messaging needs, existing libraries can go a long way toward simplifying development.

Finally, Java has an excellent track record of powering essential and scalable solutions in technology. Let's explore three of them in more depth.

Netty

Netty is a web server written in Java. It powers the web server infrastructure of companies like Facebook, Apple, Google, and Yahoo! Netty's two goals are to be portable (run in as many places as possible) and to perform (handle as many concurrent connections as possible). Building a web server requires quality implementations for web protocols, concurrency, and network management. Java has battle-tested implementations for these systems, among others. Netty's success and use can be attributed to a great developer community, ease of use, and development as a JVM project.

Apache Spark

Apache Spark is a distributed computing system for in-memory computing. Spark originated at the University of California, Berkeley, and was made freely available through the Apache Software Foundation in 2014. Companies such as Apple, Coinbase, and Capital One use Spark to power their analytics and machine learning. As with Pulsar, Spark developers utilize the JVM for its concurrency primitives and

---

5 Apache Mesos was retired from the Apache Software Foundation in 2020.

network libraries (the first versions of Spark used Netty for networking), development speed, and reliability. Spark is written in Scala, a programming language that shares the JVM with Java. The interoperability between Scala and Java allows Spark developers to build on the JVM's rich libraries.

Apache Lucene

Apache Lucene is an indexing engine that was written in Java and runs on the JVM. Lucene provides the building blocks for search systems such as Elasticsearch, Apache Solr, and CrateDB. Lucene implements the necessary algorithms to index text and perform fuzzy searching over a corpus, and it uses other critical algorithms in search. Search is something we come to expect in the 21st century. Not only can we search the entire web with tools like Google, DuckDuckGo, and Bing, but we can search our email, files on our computers, and even files across our entire presence on the web. Lucene powers the majority of search experiences we encounter on the web.

We covered the positives of the JVM and Java, but there are some negatives as well: notably, the size of JVM applications, the impact of garbage collection on application performance, and the compile times associated with large Java applications. In subsequent chapters, we'll explore how each of these downsides impacts Pulsar.

Summary

In this chapter we covered the three primary components that make up a Pulsar cluster: Pulsar brokers, Apache BookKeeper, and Apache ZooKeeper. You learned about the reasoning behind their inclusion in the project and the common thread among them: the Java virtual machine. Now that you know what Pulsar can do, you should be ready to take a closer look at how to use it. In the next few chapters, we'll discuss the interfaces and tools available in Pulsar, and how to build applications.

## CHAPTER 5

Consumers

So far, we've talked about consuming messages in Pulsar, but we haven't discussed the specifics of how messages can be consumed in Pulsar. It's worth taking a moment to specify what a consumer is in Pulsar.

A Pulsar consumer is any process that subscribes to a Pulsar topic. Consumers are typically native consumers (Java, Python, or Go processes that subscribe to topics), Pulsar Functions, Pulsar IO, or subscribers via HTTP proxy. How message brokers manage consumers has a material impact on the types of applications built on top of the messaging system. As such, Pulsar's philosophy about consuming is to be as flexible as the system can warrant. Pulsar achieves this flexibility through a novel subscription model, acknowledgment schemes, configurable consumption modes, and a tunable way to manage message age. These design decisions play a crucial role in enabling the rich applications that run on Pulsar today.

From the perspective of a messaging system, you may be asking why we aren't starting with producers before consumers. After all, we do need to get data into the system before being able to consume it. There are some good reasons to introduce consumers first, but the main reason is because there are fewer concepts to cover. Producers introduce concepts such as partitioned topics, and we'll save that until we have a better idea of some of the more rudimentary client configurations you'll find for a consumer. In this chapter you can expect a good deal more code samples.

What Does It Mean to Be a Consumer?

As I just mentioned a consumer is any process that subscribes to a Pulsar topic. A Pulsar topic is an immutable log of data. The data enters the log through a producer (or many producers) and can be consumed by a consumer (or many consumers). Figure 5-1 provides the simplest illustration of this, with one consumer and one producer consuming from a log of messages.

Figure 5-1. In this simple example of a log, one producer and one consumer consume a log with seven entries.

In this scenario, if the log were to grow from seven entries to hundreds of thousands of entries, the consumer would just continue to receive messages. This is a simple model of consumption, but it doesn't answer questions concerning the relationship between the immutable log, the producer, and the consumer. For example, what happens when the consumer is unavailable but the producer continues to publish messages? Does the consumer keep track of where they were in the log? Does the log itself keep track of it? These are questions that not only determine how programmers interact with a messaging system, but also influence what kinds of applications can be built on top of the streaming system. Pulsar handles this by providing flexibility to the end user to determine which kind of interaction the consumer (and producer) should have with the log. Pulsar refers to the mechanism by which a consumer subscribes to a topic as a *subscription*, and we'll get into how subscriptions work now.

Subscriptions

Apache Pulsar provides an abstraction and configuration for consumers, called a subscription. A subscription describes who the consumers of a topic are and how they would like to consume it. Figure 5-2 depicts how a subscription might be managed. While the topic may have many different consumers, the producer adds messages and the broker will route the messages to the correct consumers.

A subscription can be for one or more topics, and it can have one of four types of semantics. Before we jump into the subscription types in Pulsar, it's worth taking a closer look at this approach and what's required from the programmer to engage with Pulsar topics via a subscription.

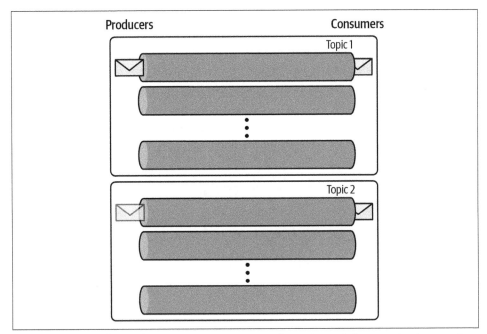

Figure 5-2. A producer places a new message into the topic, and the message is routed to an appropriate consumer.

Pulsar brokers manage the subscriptions. Since Pulsar brokers own topics or topic partitions, they are a reasonable choice for managing consumer subscriptions as well. What exactly is in a subscription? Essentially, a subscription contains a handful of metadata about the topic and the consumer that is subscribed to it, including the following:

- The topic name (or topic partition contingent on the topic)
- The name of the subscription
- The expiration details around the subscription
- The cursor for the subscription

Let's take a closer look at each of these requirements. First, including the topic name is obvious; after all, the broker needs to know what topic the consumer wishes to get data from. Each subscription has a name. When defining a consumer, the subscription name is a required field. It is a string that represents a qualified name for the subscription:

```
Consumer<byte[]> consumer = pulsarClient.newConsumer(Schema.BYTES)
            .topic(topic)
            .subscriptionName("jowanzas-subscription")
```

The expiration details of the subscription are a complex topic we will cover later in this chapter. For now, we can refer to it as the behavior Pulsar should have once it has successfully delivered a message to a subscription, or the behavior it takes if a subscriber is no longer consuming messages.

Finally, the cursor is a tracking mechanism for the Pulsar broker. It tells the broker where the consumer is in the log. You can think of a cursor as similar to the cursor in a word processor (see Figure 5-3). The cursor blinks and tells you where you are on a line. You can use the cursor to navigate the document and arrive at any point in the document.

Figure 5-3. An example of a word processor with a cursor. The cursor marks where you are in the document.

Let's take a closer look at some of the semantics of the cursor and the implementation details therein. We know a subscription manages the when and how of consumer behavior as it relates to a topic. As depicted in Figure 5-4, the subscription can manage the relationship between a topic and many consumers of that topic.

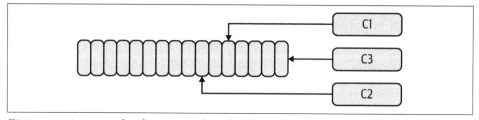

Figure 5-4. An example of a topic with multiple consumers. Each consumer has its cursor at a different point in the log.

As mentioned previously, a topic is implemented as an immutable log (or a series of immutable logs), and as such, where the cursor is in the log is a matter of where it is relative to the beginning (oldest saved message) or end (most current message) of the log. The broker keeps track of the cursor and increments it based on acknowledgment from the consumer. In the simplified example depicted in Figure 5-5, the broker sends a message to the consumer, and once it's acknowledged, the broker moves the cursor one spot.

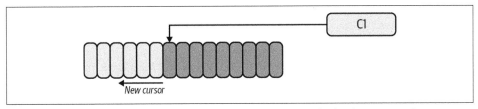

Figure 5-5. As the consumer consumes the oldest message, the broker moves the cursor closer to the most current message in the log.

How Pulsar stores the cursor for each subscription is a final detail worth exploring. As we've discussed so far in this book, Pulsar brokers are stateless. The cursor, however, is *stateful*, in that it is a representation of where a consumer is in the log. Pulsar stores each offset in a cursor ledger that is backed by Apache BookKeeper. It has all the guarantees of storage we discussed in Chapter 4. Figure 5-6 shows how the cursor ledger works. Each cursor is stored in a ledger (log), and as it updates, the new position is stored. The log is truncated over time because the current cursor is the most important component of storing the data.

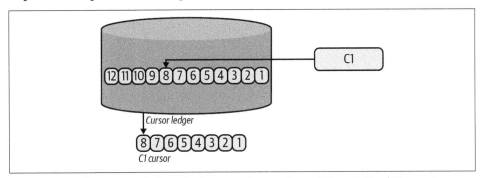

Figure 5-6. Pulsar cursor ledger. Each cursor is stored as a ledger in BookKeeper to maintain the stateless nature of the broker.

Now that you have a good understanding of subscriptions and cursors, it's time to focus on subscription types.

Exclusive

For some applications, developers may want to have only one consumer on a Pulsar topic (partitioned or unpartitioned). The exclusive subscription provides a one-to-one relationship between the consumer and the subscription. Since subscriptions are independent from a topic, multiple exclusive subscriptions can exist for one topic. To define an exclusive subscription in code, you can explicitly state you're intending an exclusive subscription. If you don't specify a subscription type, an exclusive subscription will be created:

```
Consumer consumer = client.newConsumer()
        .topic("my-topic")
        .subscriptionName("my-subscription")
        .ackTimeout(10, TimeUnit.SECONDS)
        .subscriptionType(SubscriptionType.Exclusive)// Optional
        .subscribe();
```

What happens when another consumer tries to join an exclusive subscription? If there is an active consumer, the new consumer will be rejected (see Figure 5-7).

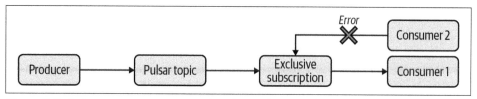

Figure 5-7. Only one consumer can utilize this exclusive subscription. When a second consumer tries it, it is rejected by the broker.

An exclusive subscription is valuable for the following reasons:

- Simplicity
- Ordering guarantees

In terms of simplicity, an exclusive subscription ensures that all messages are delivered to one consumer. For many applications, the most important aspect of the application is ensured message delivery. With fewer moving parts, it's much easier for programmers and operators to debug applications and ensure behavior.

In terms of message delivery guarantees, if strict order is a must for an application (i.e., every message needs to be processed in a strict, time-ordered sequence), an exclusive subscription is one way to help ensure ordering. As we walk through the other types of subscriptions, you'll get a better idea of why this is.

Shared

In contrast to an exclusive subscription, a shared subscription allows for multiple consumers. In a shared subscription, multiple consumers expect to receive messages from the topic in a round-robin fashion. This means there is no logical order to which messages in the topic will be delivered to a particular consumer. Figure 5-8 depicts this scenario. A shared subscription has the advantage of simplicity because you can add more consumers to the subscription without incurring any additional errors while effectively increasing the number of messages that can be consumed in a period of time.

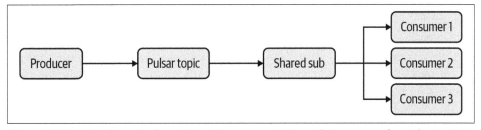

Figure 5-8. In this shared subscription, Consumers 1, 2, and 3 consume from the topic in a round-robin fashion.

Defining a consumer with a round-robin description is as simple as ensuring a subscription type as shared. As mentioned before, you can add many consumers to a shared subscription without running into any limitations. Messages will be delivered to each consumer in a round-robin fashion:

```
Consumer consumer = client.newConsumer()
        .topic("my-topic")
        .subscriptionName("my-subscription")
        .ackTimeout(10, TimeUnit.SECONDS)
        .subscriptionType(SubscriptionType.Shared)
        .subscribe();
```

There are a few limitations of a shared subscription. Following are the most notable or impactful:

- Message ordering guarantees
- Acknowledgment schemes

Since there is no concept of order or any relationship between the consumer and the topic in a shared subscription, there is no guarantee of ordering. Fortunately, for the vast majority of messaging use cases, ordering is not necessary. Acknowledgment is a complex issue that we'll look at more closely later in this chapter. However, the limitations with a shared subscription can be explained without the full context of acknowledgment.

In a shared subscription, messages are sent to consumers one at a time (serially), in round-robin fashion. This means that if the consumers must acknowledge the message, they have to acknowledge them one at a time instead of in bulk. Each acknowledgment takes network bandwidth (though not a lot) and time, so for a large number of messages, individual acknowledgment may be untenable.

Key_Shared

A Key_Shared subscription is similar to a shared subscription in that it allows for multiple consumers on a topic. The notable difference between the two is that Key_Shared subscriptions add an additional constraint in that consumers on the subscription are responsible for a key or some range of keys. Before we jump into how a Key_Shared subscription works, let's take a step back and talk about keys in Apache Pulsar.

Pulsar messages are simply bytes of data. Pulsar messages can be human readable, like a JSON (JavaScript Object Notation) blob:

```
{"name": "Jowanza", "age":100, "vehicles": ["Subaru", "Vespa", "Volkswagen"]}
```

Or they can simply be a string of nonsensical text:

```
"3q8093hdosdoaspidipas"
```

To organize these messages, a key is a piece of metadata associated with the message. Returning to our JSON blob, a key can be represented in JSON as follows:

```
{"key":"baseball player", "content":{"name": "Kerry Wood", "profession":
    "baseball player"}
```

The key acts as an organizational strategy for the data in the topic. For data formats like JSON, Avro, and Protocol Buffers (Protobuf), it's common to use a data field or key to represent the message key (as demonstrated in the preceding code). Another strategy is to use the concatenation of multiple data fields as a key.

The Key_Shared subscription works as shown in Figure 5-9, where a consumer receives messages for a key (or range of keys).

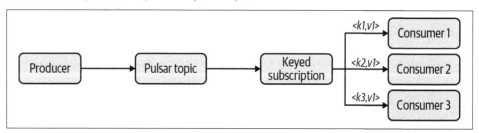

Figure 5-9. In this Key_Shared subscription, Consumer 1 receives all messages for K1, Consumer 2 receives all messages for K2, and Consumer 3 receives all messages for K3.

In this example, we're only looking at three keys that conveniently match with three consumers. In real applications, such a clean matching of keys with consumers is unlikely. In Pulsar, there are two ways to handle this problem: have Pulsar manage the process or implement a solution to the process. Let's discuss each solution in more detail.

When defining a Key_Shared subscription, it's necessary to define both the subscription type and the specific policy, or how the keys should be distributed among the consumers:

```
Consumer < String > consumer = client.newConsumer(Schema.JSON)
    .subscriptionMode(SubscriptionMode.Durable)
    .topic("our-topic")
    .consumerName("auto-hashed-consumer")
    .subscriptionName("auto-hashed")
    .subscriptionType(SubscriptionType.Key_Shared)
    .keySharedPolicy(KeySharedPolicy.autoSplitHashRange())
    .subscribe();
```

The way the keys are distributed among the consumers in the subscription is determined by the keySharedPolicy. To understand why this is significant, we need to understand the idea behind consistent hashing in distributed systems. In the shared subscription model, each message is routed to each consumer, as shown in Figure 5-10.

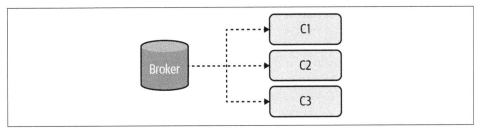

Figure 5-10. In this shared subscription, consumers C1, C2, and C3 receive messages in a round-robin fashion.

The weakness of the shared subscription has to do with ordering guarantees. Since no set of messages is the responsibility of a consumer (or group of consumers), we cannot say anything definitive about the messages. To improve the ordering guarantee around message processing, we need some kind of guarantee that a group of messages is processed by an individual consumer. The key in a Pulsar message can be used as an identifier for a message, and it can link the message to a specific consumer. However, it must guarantee that the message reaches the same consumer every time.

Pulsar provides two approaches to provide this guarantee: auto hashing and sticky hashing. *Hashing* is a process for converting arbitrary values into values of a fixed size. An example is converting a name into a number. Since keys on Pulsar messages can be any arbitrary value, hashing provides a way to convert that value into a numerical value that each consumer can use. With each key converted into a hashed value, consumers to the subscription are then assigned a hash value range (see Figure 5-11). In a sticky hash, the consumer range values are set manually by the client. The ranges are "sticky" in that all hashes in a particular range go to one consumer.

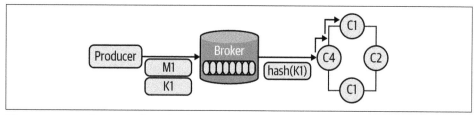

Figure 5-11. In this Key_Shared subscription, a producer produces a message with K1 and that key is hashed and shared with a consumer in the hash range.

For a consumer in the sticky hash range, you can set the policy based on a range value. In the following example, I used the node count:

```
consumer = client.newConsumer(Schema.STRING)
    .subscriptionMode(SubscriptionMode.Durable)
    .topic("persistent://public/default/sticky")
    .consumerName("my-consumer")
    .subscriptionName("sticky-sub")
    .subscriptionType(SubscriptionType.Key_Shared)
    .keySharedPolicy(KeySharedPolicy.stickyHashRange().ranges(range))
    .subscribe();
```

An alternative to the sticky hash is the auto hash. In this mode, Pulsar automatically balances the hash ranges across available consumers. The auto hash uses consistent hashing (*https://oreil.ly/41G34*) to ensure that the load remains equally distributed as consumers add and drop from the subscription (see Figure 5-12). Upsides to auto hashing are that you can "set it and forget it" and it enables delivery to the right consumer (see Figure 5-13).

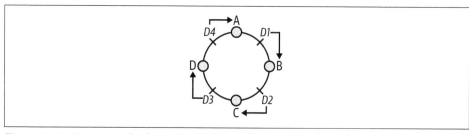

Figure 5-12. Consistent hashing. For Nodes A, B, C, and D, Messages D1–D4 are placed within the hashing ring according to the hash range of the consumer.

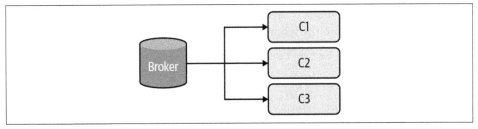

Figure 5-13. In this Key_Shared subscription, the broker knows exactly which consumer should get a message based on the key.

In the event of a failure, the hash ring will remove the failing node and the keys will continue to move in a clockwise fashion (see Figure 5-14).

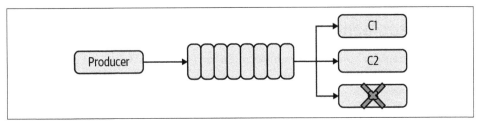

Figure 5-14. When a consumer goes offline in a Key_Shared subscription, the "ring" will change and C1 and C2 will receive new messages.

Failover

A failover subscription allows for multiple consumers to connect to the topic. The broker chooses a "leader" (typically the first consumer to connect to the subscription), and messages are delivered to that consumer as long as the consumer and leader are connected, as depicted in Figure 5-15. If that consumer goes offline, the messages are delivered to a backup consumer. It is important to note that while there are standby consumers in this subscription mode, only one consumer at a time will receive messages. Ordering can be guaranteed in this subscription model, and cumulative acknowledgments are possible in this mode (more on this soon).

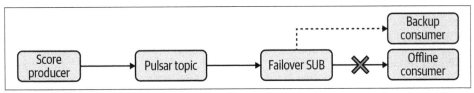

Figure 5-15. A failover subscription. Once the active consumer goes offline, the messages in the subscription are shared with the backup consumer.

A failover subscription is defined by setting the subscriptionType to Subscription Type.Failover, as shown in the following code snippet:

```
Consumer consumer = client.newConsumer()
        .topic("my-topic")
        .subscriptionName("my-subscription")
        .ackTimeout(10, TimeUnit.SECONDS)
        .subscriptionType(SubscriptionType.Failover)
        .subscribe();
```

The use case for a failover subscription is an application where strict ordering and quick processing of messages are equally important.

Now that we've covered all the subscription modes in Pulsar, we can move on to another important concept: acknowledgments.

Acknowledgments

Acknowledgments are a vital mechanism in Pulsar. An acknowledgment is a communication sent from a consumer to a Pulsar broker validating that a specific message or group of messages was consumed. Pulsar supports two types of acknowledgments: individual and cumulative. This section will cover both.

Acknowledgments (or acks) are used in every contemporary messaging system. In traditional pub/sub systems, an acknowledgment tells the broker that it is OK to delete a message because it's no longer needed by the consumer. In Pulsar, acknowledgments serve a similar but slightly more nuanced purpose.

Individual Ack

By default, each message within a Pulsar topic needs acknowledgment. As a consumer processes a message, it sends an acknowledgment to the broker (see Figure 5-16). For some subscription modes, the individual ack is the only ack strategy available.

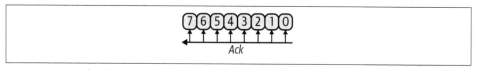

Figure 5-16. Individual ack. Each message in the subscription must be acknowledged by the broker serially.

Individual acks ensure that each message in the subscription has been consumed. All subscription modes support individual acks, as shown in Table 5-1.

Individual acks in code require acknowledging a received message, as shown here:

```
String data = new String(message.getData());
log.info("Consumer received : " + data);
consumer.acknowledge(message);
message = consumer.receive(100, TimeUnit.MILLISECONDS);
```

An alternative to acknowledging each message individually is to acknowledge batches of them. There are some advantages of batch acknowledgment, which we'll cover in the next section.

Table 5-1. Subscription modes and their support for individual ack

Subscription mode	Supports individual ack
Exclusive	Yes
Shared	Yes
Key_Shared	Yes
Failover	Yes

Cumulative Ack

A cumulative acknowledgment acknowledges messages at an offset in the stream, and all messages delivered before it are acknowledged (automatically) as well (see Figure 5-17). This strategy reduces the number of acknowledgments and enables the consumers to operate in a "batch" workflow. Table 5-2 summarizes the subscription modes supporting cumulative acks.

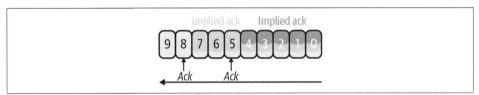

Figure 5-17. Cumulative ack. The consumer acknowledges a message at a specific cursor (offset) and all messages before that point in the cursor are considered acknowledged by the broker.

Table 5-2. Subscription modes and their support for cumulative ack

Subscription type	Supports cumulative ack
Exclusive	Yes
Shared	No
Key_Shared	Yes
Failover	Yes

Schemas

Schemas are an optional but influential part of the Apache Pulsar ecosystem. Users can enable both schemas and schema validation for topics. When a schema is enabled, producers must adhere to it, and consumers will know what to expect from the data's shape. In Chapter 6, we'll cover the Pulsar schema registry and end-to-end workflows; here, we'll focus on consumers and how they interact with schemas in Apache Pulsar.

Consumer Schema Management

Pulsar consumers can interact with schemas through two mechanisms. Suppose a schema is set on a topic, and schema validation is enforced. In that case, all a consumer needs to do is consume messages and deserialize them according to the schema (send the schema with the message). Alternatively, if a schema is not set on a topic, a consumer can enable it and register it with the schema registry (see Figure 5-18). At first glance, it may seem dangerous to allow a consumer to add a schema. After all, the consumer is supposed to consume messages and should not determine the shape of messages. However, since the consumer is part of the entire message lifecycle, safely enabling consumers to register schemas has some positive ramifications, which we'll cover in Chapter 6.

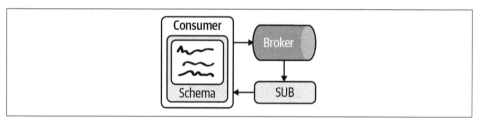

Figure 5-18. A consumer retrieves a schema to consume from a subscription.

Consumption Modes

A theme throughout this book is that Apache Pulsar is intentionally configurable. In addition to configuring subscriptions, schemas, and acknowledgments, Pulsar end users can also configure consumption. Pulsar is concerned with message order and delivery guarantees, and it seems natural that consuming the messages serially (one at a time) may be best. However, providing flexibility on how messages get delivered to Pulsar topics and eventually consumed enables richer interactions and more scalability.

Batching

The batching strategy for messages will be covered in depth in Chapter 6. For now, we'll focus on what batching is and the implications for batching on a Pulsar consumer.

When a Pulsar producer publishes messages to a Pulsar consumer, the messages can be published one at a time. There are some unambiguous upsides of publishing messages one at a time, but there are also some downsides. The main downside is that connecting to a Pulsar broker is not a free operation. For producers that need to publish many messages per second, it may be unfeasible or dangerous to open and close connections that rapidly.

Additionally, in most cases sending messages immediately and serially is not beneficial to the entire application flow. A reasonable strategy would be to send Pulsar messages based on a maximum message volume or time period. In Pulsar, this message delivery mechanism is known as batching.

How does batching impact a consumer? In most cases, batching does not have a material impact on the consumer. As discussed in the previous section, each message in the batch needs to be acknowledged by the consumer. Before Pulsar 2.8, a consumer would acknowledge an entire batch of messages. In most cases, this is precisely the behavior you want; however, what if a consumer dies after consuming all but the last two messages in a batch? The consumer would send a negative acknowledgment for the batch and could process messages from that batch again (see Figure 5-19).

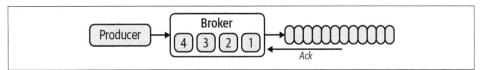

Figure 5-19. In this representation of consumer batch consumption, a consumer sends a negative acknowledgment for the batch and can process messages from that batch again.

In Pulsar 2.8, a batch index was introduced. This index gives the consumer more flexibility in determining precisely where in the batch it ended its processing. This index removes the complexity of managing the index for the consumer and provides transparency for the broker.

Chunking

An alternative mechanism to batching messages in Pulsar is chunking. Instead of configuring a consumer to send a message based on a time interval or the maximum number of messages, chunking splits larger messages into chunks. In this section, we'll discuss how a chunked message impacts a consumer. The chunking mechanism will be covered in detail in Chapter 6.

When messages are chunked, they arrive at a consumer chunked with metadata to know the chunk's number of partitions. The consumer awaits each part of the chunk to stitch it back together before the acknowledgment (see Figure 5-20). Chunking is essential because it provides a mechanism for consuming large messages in Pulsar without causing cascading failures. Additionally, Pulsar provides this functionality transparently to the consumer, which receives metadata about chunked messages for proper processing and acknowledgment.

Figure 5-20. When chunking for large payloads, messages are split before being sent to the consumer.

Advanced Configuration

Throughout this chapter, we've discussed Pulsar's customization. With each release, the Pulsar developers enable more customization to enable richer interactions and expand the number of use cases for which Pulsar is suitable. To round out this chapter on consumers, we'll cover two additional configurations and features possible with Pulsar: delayed messages and time to live (TTL).

Delayed Messages

In Chapter 3, we talked about Iterable, a marketing automation company that rebuilt its backend system to utilize Apache Pulsar. One use case cited by Iterable is the necessity to delay messages for future delivery for email automation purposes. Pulsar enables delayed message functionality. Pulsar delayed messages only work in a shared subscription mode. When a message is marked as delayed, the `DelayedDelivery Tracker` configuration tracks the message and ensures that it is delivered at the delayed time.

From the consumer perspective, when the delayed message arrives in the Pulsar topic, `DelayedDeliveryTracker` will cause a timeout when the consumer attempts to consume the message (see Figure 5-21). The delayed message illustrates Pulsar's features and modularity, working together to provide an elegant experience outside Pulsar's initial design scope. Delayed messages have use cases in notification systems, email systems, and administration systems, to name a few.

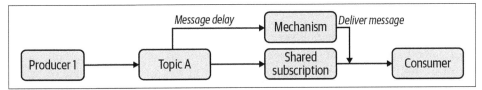

Figure 5-21. Delayed messages in Pulsar. The Pulsar broker manages delaying the message by storing it in BookKeeper temporarily and resurfacing it when needed.

Delayed messages are consumed by Pulsar consumers like any other message. From the producer side, setting a delayed message with the client library looks like this:

```
// message to be delivered at the configured delay interval of 5 minutes
producer.newMessage().deliverAfter(5L, TimeUnit.Minute).
    value("Hello Moto!").send();
```

Retention Policy

At this point, you may be wondering what Pulsar does with messages that have already been acknowledged by all subscribers of a topic. If every subscriber acknowledges a message, this is an indication that Pulsar should no longer store the message. We would store the message for replaying the topic, for new subscriptions, and for other long-term storage needs. Pulsar provides two ways for an operator to configure the storage of acknowledged messages.

Using the Pulsar Admin CLI, you can set the retention for acknowledged messages by time or by size. This configuration is set at a namespace level and all topics in that namespace adhere to the policy. Here is an example of setting the policy:

```
$ pulsar-admin namespaces set-retention my-tenant/new-namespace \
  --size 10G \
  --time 3h
```

In this command, we set the namespace limit to 10 GB of space and the time limit to three hours. Table 5-3 summarizes the range of values for this API.

Table 5-3. Retention policy behavior in pulsar

Time limit (hours)	Size limit (GB)	Behavior
−1	−1	Stores data forever. No limit on size or time.
−1	> 0	Stores data until the size limit is reached.
> 0	−1	Stores data only based on the time limit.
0	0	Message retention for acknowledged messages is disabled.
0	> 0	Not valid.
> 0	0	Not valid.
> 0	> 0	Size or time limit (whichever is reached first).

Backlog Quota

Many of the applications that utilize a real-time backend such as Apache Pulsar have requirements about how long messages that enter the system are relevant. For example, in a smart-home system, a messaging platform that handles the state of lights (whether the lights are on, off, or dimmed) may run behind in message consumption. If the consumer has thousands of state changes to catch up on, it may make more sense to ignore older messages and begin reacting to newly arriving ones.

By default, Apache Pulsar stores all unacknowledged messages. For most cases, it's hard to find fault with this default behavior. However, when the consumer is running behind, it may make sense to drop those unacknowledged messages in favor of newly arriving ones. The backlog quota provides a similar interface for managing unacknowledged messages that the retention policy does for acknowledged messages.

Backlog quotas are set on a namespace level and apply to all the topics in the namespace. You can use the Pulsar Admin CLI to set the backlog quote for the namespace:

```
$ pulsar-admin namespaces set-backlog-quota my-tenant/my-namespace \
   --limit 2G \
   --limitTime 36000 \
   --policy producer_request_hold
```

Similar to the retention policy, you can limit the size and time that you keep unacknowledged messages. You can also set a policy that dictates how the system will behave if the quotas are reached, as shown in Table 5-4.

Table 5-4. Policies and their behavior

Policy	Behavior
producer_request_hold	The broker will hold and not persist the producer request payload.
producer_exception	The broker will disconnect from the client by throwing an exception.
consumer_backlog_eviction	The broker will begin discarding backlog messages.

In addition to backlog quotes and retention policies, Pulsar also allows you to set a message expiry or time to live (TTL) at a namespace level. This is useful if you want to just set a strictly time-based mechanism for your unacknowledged messages, as shown in the following code:

```
$ pulsar-admin namespaces set-message-ttl my-tenant/my-namespace \
   --messageTTL 120 # In seconds
```

Backlog quotas and retention policies may feel similar, but they serve very different purposes. Backlog quotas are all about the behavior of unacknowledged messages, and retention policies are all about how long to keep data after it's been acknowledged. The good news is that both can be set on a namespace level and both can be set to infinite if it's too hard to decide on a TTL. Table 5-5 summarizes the differences between backlog quotas and retention policies.

Table 5-5. A summary of backlog quotas and retention policies

	Backlog Quotas	Retention Policies
Time based	Yes (optional)	Yes (optional)
Size based	Yes (optional)	Yes (optional)
Set at	Namespace	Namespace
Behavior when met	Configurable	Delete messages
Acked or unacked	Unacked	Acked

Configuring a Consumer

We've spent most of this chapter discussing features available to Pulsar consumers. In this section, we'll discuss how to configure a consumer. As mentioned previously, Pulsar has officially supported client libraries in Java, Python, and Go. Here we'll focus on the Java library, and discuss Python and Go when it's easier to illustrate a client library feature with those languages. We'll go through each option for configuring your consumer and what that configuration change will affect.

Replay

One of the selling points you'll hear about systems like Apache Pulsar, Kafka, and others is that they offer the ability to *replay* a topic. This means a consumer can consume messages in the order in which they arrived at the topic (or topic partition for partitioned topics). In Pulsar there are three ways you can replay data in a topic:

- Manually set the cursor for a consumer back to the earliest offset (see Figure 5-22)

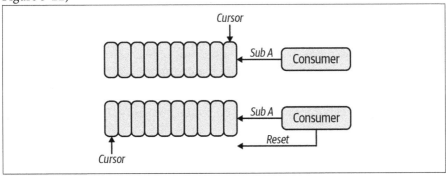

Figure 5-22. A consumer resets the cursor for the subscription. This action would set the cursor back to the earliest stored message in BookKeeper.

- Negatively acknowledge a message (see Figure 5-23)

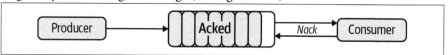

Figure 5-23. A consumer negatively acknowledges the latest message in the subscription. Unlike all other messages in the subscription, this message is treated as if it wasn't ever sent to the consumer.

- Reset the cursor for the subscription via the Pulsar CLI or API (see Figure 5-24)

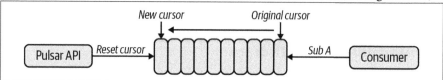

Figure 5-24. A Pulsar Admin API user resets a subscription to the earliest offset. The consumers on this subscription will start to consume messages from the earliest point stored in BookKeeper.

We can manually set the cursor by using the consumer library:

```
import org.apache.pulsar.client.api.MessageId;
import org.apache.pulsar.client.api.Reader;

Reader<byte[]> reader = pulsarClient.newReader()
    .topic("read-from-topic")
    .startMessageId(MessageId.earliest) // get data at earliest offset
    .create();

while (true) {
    Message message = reader.readNext();

    // Get messages after this point
}
```

A negative acknowledgment tells the Pulsar broker that your subscription was not able to process the message. You can use the consumer API to negatively acknowledge a message and it will be queued for redelivery, as shown here:

```
Consumer<byte[]> consumer =
    Client
        .newConsumer()
        .subscriptionType(SubscriptionType.Key_Shared)
        .subscriptionName("abc-sub")
        .topic("abbc")
        .subscribe();
while (true) {
    Message<byte[]> message = consumer.receive(100, TimeUnit.MILLISECONDS);
```

```
      if (message != null) {
        System.out.println(new String(message.getData()));
        consumer.negativeAcknowledge(message);
      }
```

The final alternative for resetting a cursor for a subscription is to do so from the administrative APIs in Pulsar. You can use the Pulsar CLI to do so with the following command:

```
$ pulsar-admin topics reset-cursor topic a --subscription my-subscription
```

Or you can use the Admin API:

```
POST/admin/persistent/:tenant/:namespace/
      :destination/subscription/:subName/resetcursor
```

Replay comes is useful for a number of scenarios, including the following:

- Allowing new consumers to read the entire history of a topic
- Auditing a topic
- Stream processing

Dead Letter Topics

In the traditional messaging world, a dead letter queue is a queue in which messages that are unable to be processed to the normal flow are sent. Messages may not be processed for several reasons:

- The message does not adhere to the shared schema and cannot be processed by the consumer.
- The consumer was not able to process the message in time.
- The consumer failed when processing the message.

In Pulsar, dead letter queues can serve the same purpose. A dead letter is a topic that is preconfigured to tell the broker where messages should go in the event of a failure to process. In Pulsar there are two ways messages can fail:

- Negative acknowledgment (telling the broker you do not want to acknowledge the message)
- Acknowledgment timeouts (not processing the message with time left)

You can define a dead letter topic when setting up a subscription:

```
Consumer<byte[]> consumer = pulsarClient.newConsumer(Schema.BYTES)
              .topic(topic)
              .subscriptionName("hello-moto")
              .subscriptionType(SubscriptionType.Shared)
              .deadLetterPolicy(DeadLetterPolicy.builder()
```

```
                .maxRedeliverCount(maxRedeliveryCount)
                .build())
        .subscribe();
```

By default, the dead letter topic will have a name that looks like this:

```
<topicname>-<subscriptionname>-DLQ
```

You can set the dead letter topic name manually if you wish:

```
Consumer<byte[]> consumer = pulsarClient.newConsumer(Schema.BYTES)
                .topic(topic)
                .subscriptionName("hello-moto")
                .subscriptionType(SubscriptionType.Shared)
                .deadLetterPolicy(DeadLetterPolicy.builder()
                        .maxRedeliverCount(maxRedeliveryCount)
                        .deadLetterTopic("hello-moto-dlq")
                        .build())
                .subscribe();
```

It's important to remember that dead letter topics are on a subscription basis. If one subscription encounters a problem and requires dead lettering, others are likely to as well.

Retry Letter Topics

For some applications, automatically retrying a negatively acknowledged message may be appropriate. Retry letter topics provide a mechanism for a consumer to configure this behavior. A retry letter topic requires the following:

- Retry must be enabled to support this style of delivery.
- A topic must be available to store the messages queued to be retried.

You can define a retry letter topic with the Pulsar client library:

```
Consumer<byte[]> consumer = pulsarClient.newConsumer(Schema.BYTES)
    .topic(topic)
    .subscriptionName("scary-hours")
    .subscriptionType(SubscriptionType.Shared)
    .enableRetry(true)
    .receiverQueueSize(100)
    .deadLetterPolicy(DeadLetterPolicy.builder()
      .maxRedeliverCount(maxRedeliveryCount)
      .retryLetterTopic("persistent://my-property/my-ns/scary-hours-retry-Retry")
      .build())
    .subscriptionInitialPosition(SubscriptionInitialPosition.Earliest)
    .subscribe();
```

Summary

In this chapter, we covered what it means to be a consumer in Apache Pulsar. More than simply reading messages off a queue, consumers are where the "rubber meets the road" for streaming applications. We discussed many topics, including:

- How messages are chunked to consumers
- Acknowledgment strategies for consumers
- Pulsar's subscription model
- Some techniques for configuring Pulsar brokers

You should now be equipped with enough information to tackle the other side of the equation: how the producer gets data into Pulsar.

## CHAPTER 6

Producers

In Chapter 5, we discussed the philosophy of consuming in Apache Pulsar. Producing messages is the other half of the equation, and it's worth spending some time talking about what responsibilities producers have in a Pulsar system. In general, Pulsar producers control the messages' schema, routing strategy, encryption, and compression. The producer is the authority figure for messages and is mainly removed from the consumption of messages.

As you learned so far, Pulsar client libraries contain many knobs for tuning performance and allowing the end user to manage the flow of messages. Still, much of the complexity behind ensuring reliability in Pulsar happens with the brokers and in ZooKeeper and BookKeeper. In this chapter, we'll cover some of the semantics of Pulsar producers and standard settings.

Synchronous Producers

Synchronous producers await acknowledgment from the Pulsar broker before considering a message or packet as having been "sent." Synchronous producers provide the strongest guarantee around message delivery but have some implications for performance and may not be perfect for every application topology.

Figure 6-1 depicts an illustration of a sync send operation in Pulsar. When Message 1 (M1) is acknowledged by the Pulsar broker, M2 is sent, and so on.

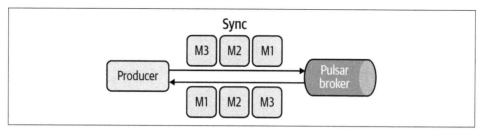

Figure 6-1. A synchronous producer in Apache Pulsar. The producer sends messages M1, M2, and M3, and the broker acknowledges each message.

From the producer's perspective, you can be confident that every message is safely stored (and replicated) in Pulsar. Sync might be necessary for overall guarantee of message delivery for mission-critical or transactional systems. However, sending messages individually and awaiting broker confirmation comes at a cost: communicating over the network takes time, and a Pulsar broker may be unable to acknowledge the message at a predictable latency, thereby causing problems downstream (see Figure 6-2).

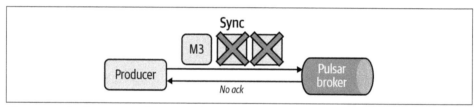

Figure 6-2. In the sync send setting, if messages are not acknowledged by the broker, it is as though they were never sent.

Should you use sync send in your Pulsar topology? The answer is that it depends on your system's throughput and whether you can wait for each message to be acknowledged.

Consider a producer that is using sync send. This producer manages a set number of requests per second, and only one message can be sent to the Pulsar brokers at a time. As new concurrent upstream requests come along, the producer has to manage those connections while still awaiting full sync downstream. This process can result in a situation where all upstream processes are waiting for the producer and there is latency across the system.

Fortunately, we can treat this process as equal parts art and science. Chapter 12 covers some metrics you can use to determine latencies across your topic topology and determine whether send sync is appropriate for your use case.

Asynchronous Producers

Async producers send their messages to the Pulsar broker as a background task. The producer keeps an internal blocking queue of messages, and each message is sent to the Pulsar broker "out of band." By offloading messages to a background task, the producer isn't blocked and can process new messages and other tasks (see Figure 6-3).

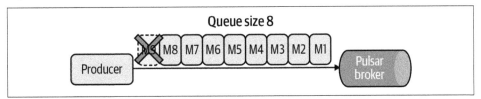

Figure 6-3. Send queue size. This queue size is configurable and keeps track of messages that the producer has sent to the Pulsar broker.

The majority of messaging use cases can benefit from async production. The async paradigm is popular in networked programming, where network call latency is only predictable within a distribution. This means that tail latency can exceed the average, and blocking network calls can make an entire application feel slow. Pulsar brokers are not immune to network communication problems, and a producer may block on a slow network call, causing a cascading effect in the application pipeline. The async send separates the networking needed to send the message from the producer's other responsibilities and only blocks when needed (see Figure 6-4).

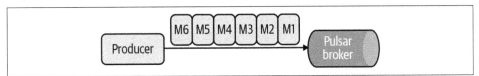

Figure 6-4. An async producer. Messages are queued and sent to the Pulsar broker out of band rather than directly, one message at a time.

Producer Routing

Before we jump into why a producer would route messages, we should talk about partitioned topics. A partitioned topic is a topic that splits or partitions its ownership across multiple brokers. Partitioning a topic affects one crucial function: performance. By partitioning a topic, you increase the number of brokers that can receive messages for that topic and increase the overall number of messages per period ingested by Pulsar. In contrast to Kafka, where every topic is partitioned, in Pulsar, topics are not partitioned by default.

How a topic is partitioned is another essential consideration. Typically, topics are partitioned by a *key*, or a value in the message payloads with some identifying characteristic. Once the partitioning process has been established, the producer needs to route each message to the proper partition for a topic. In Apache Pulsar, this is where producer routing comes into play.

Pulsar supports three routing schemes for partitioned topics:

- Round-robin routing
- Single partition routing
- Custom partition routing

Round-Robin Routing

Round-robin routing acts as a load balancer. It sends messages to partitions in order and has the advantage of simplicity (see Figure 6-5). Round robin is a common routing strategy because it doesn't require much configuration or forethought, yet allows for outstanding performance.

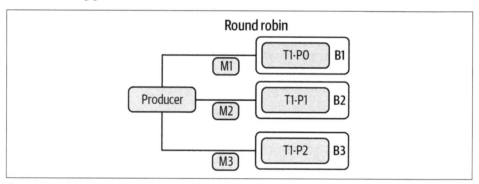

Figure 6-5. The producer routes messages to brokers in a round-robin fashion.

You can configure round robin with or without a key. Table 6-1 summarizes the differences between the two approaches.

Table 6-1. Configuring a round-robin router with and without a key

Approach	Consequences
Key specified	When a key is specified, the broker will hash the keys and route them to the same partition (discussed in "Key_Shared" on page 68).
No key specified	When no key is specified, the broker uses the batch settings to determine which partition gets which messages.

You can define the partitioning with the Pulsar Java client like this:

```
String pulsarBrokerRootUrl = "pulsar://localhost:6650";
String topic = "persistent://my-tenant/my-namespace/ggc";

PulsarClient pulsarClient = PulsarClient.builder()
                .serviceUrl(pulsarBrokerRootUrl)
                .build();
Producer<byte[]> producer = pulsarClient.newProducer()
        .topic(topic)
        .messageRoutingMode(MessageRoutingMode.RoundRobin)
        .create();

producer.newMessage().key("my-key")
                .value("A letter to my unborn".getBytes())
                .send();
```

Single Partition Routing

Single partition routing provides an even simpler mechanism: it routes all messages to a single partition (see Figure 6-6). This mode is similar to an unpartitioned topic. Essentially, one broker is in charge of all messages. This partitioning mode occurs when *SinglePartition* is selected and no key is provided. When a key is provided, the behavior reverts to a consistent hashing scheme similar to round-robin routing. Table 6-2 summarizes these differences.

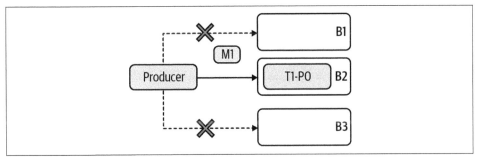

Figure 6-6. In this configuration, the producer sends all messages to a single partition owned by a single broker. If a key is supplied, it is hashed and messages are routed to specific partitions.

Table 6-2. Single partition routing with and without a key

Key	Behavior
Key specified	Keys are hashed and assigned to particular producers.
No key specified	A single broker (partition) receives all the messages.

You can define a single partition using the Java Pulsar client library:

```
String pulsarBrokerRootUrl = "pulsar://localhost:6650";
String topic = "persistent://my-tenant/my-namespace/ggc";

PulsarClient pulsarClient = PulsarClient.builder()
                .serviceUrl(pulsarBrokerRootUrl)
                .build();
Producer<byte[]> producer = pulsarClient.newProducer()
            .topic(topic)
            .messageRoutingMode(MessageRoutingMode.SinglePartition)
            .create();

producer.newMessage().key("my-key")
                .value("A letter to my unborn"
                .getBytes()).send();
```

Custom Partition Routing

Custom partition routing provides a mechanism for the producer to describe how messages should be routed to partitions. You can use a custom partition for routing based on specific keys or other metadata within a message. For a simple example, you may want to route every message with a specific key to a specific partition (see Figure 6-7), or route messages with a specific version of a schema to a specific partition.

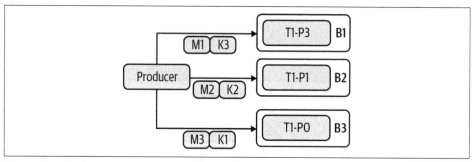

Figure 6-7. In this custom partition, the producer implements logic to ensure that data is sent to a specific partition.

Defining your own partition in Pulsar is simple if you are using the Java client library. You need to implement the MessageRouter interface, which has one method called choosePartition. It looks like this:

```
public interface MessageRouter extends Serializable {
    int choosePartition(Message msg);
}
```

With this interface, we can implement a router that randomly assigns partitions 6–10:

```
public class RandomRouter implements MessageRouter {
    public int choosePartition(Message msg) {
        Random ran = new Random();
int x = ran.nextInt(6) + 5;

        return x;
    }
}
```

Now we can use our router to route messages on a partitioned topic:

```
String pulsarBrokerRootUrl = "pulsar://localhost:6650";
String topic = "persistent://my-tenant/my-cluster-my-namespace/ggc";

PulsarClient pulsarClient = PulsarClient.builder()
                .serviceUrl(pulsarBrokerRootUrl)
                .build();
Producer<byte[]> producer = pulsarClient.newProducer()
        .topic(topic)
        .messageRouter(new RandomRouter())
        .create();
producer.send("Hello, Moto".getBytes());
```

Finally, we can use message keys to route:

```
// If the message has a key, it supersedes the round robin routing policy
    if (msg.hasKey()) {
        return signSafeMod(hash.makeHash(msg.getKey()),
        topicMetadata.numPartitions());
    }

    if (isBatchingEnabled) { // if batching is enabled,
                            // choose partition on `partitionSwitchMs` boundary.
        long currentMs = clock.millis();
        return signSafeMod(currentMs / partitionSwitchMs + startPtnIdx,
            topicMetadata.numPartitions());
    } else {
        return signSafeMod(PARTITION_INDEX_UPDATER.getAndIncrement(this),
            topicMetadata.numPartitions());
    }
```

Producer Configuration

Pulsar producers are highly configurable. Throughout this chapter, we've interacted with several code examples that utilize configurations for Pulsar producers. Now we'll go through each configuration and expound a bit on their meaning as well as provide a reference section for ourselves in the future.

topicName

Pulsar topic names can have any character except the forward slash (/). By default, this configuration is null and will not submit any messages to the consumer. Generally, topic names are hyphenated, as in "my-topic." However, this naming convention is just a suggestion, and organizations can choose whatever naming convention they want.

producerName

The producer name is a string that identifies the producer. This name needs to be unique within a Pulsar distribution. One convention I've seen for producerName is *<team>.<application>*. As with topicName, there are no enforced naming schemes.

sendTimeoutMs

This configuration sets the maximum amount of time (in milliseconds) the producer should wait for a Pulsar broker to acknowledge a packet. By default, this setting is 30,000 ms (30 seconds). We talked about sync send earlier in this chapter, and 30 seconds is far too high for any application in that scenario. For the async case, 30 seconds is a reasonable choice.

blockIfQueueFull

This configuration sets the behavior for the outgoing queue in the async send scenario. If set to true, when an additional message attempts to add to the queue it is blocked, rather than failing. If set to false, when additional messages attempt to add to the queue a ProducerQueueIsFullError is returned. In these cases, the producer needs to deal with the error immediately. By default, this parameter is set to false. On some further examination, it is a reasonable decision to set this parameter to false. It is much more transparent and forces producers to consider faults in their programs.

maxPendingMessages

This configuration sets the maximum number of messages queued for processing in the async send mode. The default for this setting is 1,000, and this value can be set to any integer.

maxPendingMessagesAcrossPartitions

For partitioned topics, this value is the sum of max pending messages across all partitions. This configuration is necessary because it clarifies communication health between the brokers and the producer. For partitioned topics, variance in the acknowledgment speed is typical, and keeping track of the overall health of message sync between all partitions can help when designing a producer. By default, the `max PendingMessagesAcrossPartitions` value is set to 5,000, but there are several reasons to tune that value.

messageRoutingMode

For partitioned topics, Pulsar supports three routing modes:

- Round robin
- Single partition
- Custom partition

We described each of these routing modes in detail in "Producer Routing" on page 87.

hashingScheme

`hashingScheme` is a function used to determine how to route messages in a partitioned topic. By default, this configuration is set to `JavaStringHash`, which provides a basic string hashing algorithm on the message for routing. The two alternatives are `pulsar.Murmur3_32Hash` and `pulsar.BoostHash`. Both have some performance implications (they can be much faster) and have some other implications regarding uniqueness. Hashing (*https://oreil.ly/0Z5kQ*) is a complex topic that is beyond the scope of this book, so I have included a footnote for further reading.[1]

cryptoFailureAction

This configuration dictates the behavior of the producer of encryption failure. By default, if the producer fails to encrypt the message, the message won't be sent to the Pulsar broker. The alternative is that the unencrypted message is still sent to the broker. Also by default, Pulsar wants to encrypt each message. The setting illustrates this behavior to fail to send when encryption is not successful. While this book is not about security, security is an essential consideration in a messaging system. Ensuring that only sanctioned parties can read the data is a sensible default.

batchingMaxPublishDelayMicros

This configuration sets the maximum number of microseconds of delay a producer should wait to send a batch to a Pulsar broker. By default, this is set to 100 microseconds.

---

1 Kelly Brown, "The Dangers of Weak Hashes," SANS Whitepaper (November 2013). *https://oreil.ly/d7rcc.*

batchingMaxMessages

This configuration sets a maximum batch size for a producer. When the limit is reached, the producer sends a batch of messages to a Pulsar broker.

batchingEnabled

By default, batching with 1,000 messages or 1 ms is enabled. Since the Pulsar broker manages to decompose a batch for subscribers, you can set this configuration much higher if your use case requires it.

compressionType

By default, compression is off on Pulsar topics. Pulsar supports four compression algorithms, and it's worth going through each one to understand their trade-offs. This section is not a primer on compression algorithm design; instead, it provides a glimpse of what each compression algorithm has to offer and why you might consider one over the other or none of them at all.

Before we dive into each algorithm, let's consider why we would compress messages in the first place. The only reason is because of disk space. Thinking about Pulsar as a record system or a system that stores all messages indefinitely, disk space is at a premium. Compression of 20% to 40% (what these algorithms offer) can save millions of dollars in storage costs over time.

There are three essential things to consider with a compression algorithm: how quickly it can compress data given the hardware that's available, how long it takes to transfer the data, and how long it takes to decompress it on the other end when needed.

Pulsar supports the following compression algorithms. Each algorithm has some trade-offs based on specific use cases, as summarized in the following list:

LZ4
> LZ4's focus is to provide the best performance on the smallest amount of computing resources. It's suitable for a wide array of applications.

ZLIB
> ZLIB has similar advantages to LZ4. However, it is focused on ecosystem compatibility. Many programming languages have ZLIB implementations, making it a good choice for compression in a polyglot ecosystem.

ZSTD
> ZSTD is a compression algorithm focused on delivering the smallest final file size at the cost of requiring more compute power to get there.

Snappy

Snappy is a compression algorithm that sacrifices optimization in final file size for the overall speed of compression. Snappy is typically used for data analytics workloads such as those found with Parquet files.

Schema on Write

In Chapter 5, we discussed how Pulsar topics are schema optional. Philosophically, a producer is best positioned to declare a schema and may even provide that on delivering data to the topic. The idea of creating a schema for data before storing it is called *schema on write*. Schema on write is a defensive technique and is inflexible. Once the schema is declared and enforced on the broker level, changing it requires producers and consumers to move to a new schema. In this section, we'll cover the following:

- Creating schemas
- Schema enforcement
- Supported schemas

Using the Schema Registry

By default, Pulsar uses Apache BookKeeper for schema storage. Pulsar does support third-party schema registries as well, but for this book we'll stick to the built-in registry.[2]

A schema is automatically created when a typed producer (see Figure 6-8) publishes messages to a topic in Pulsar. However, for any topic, you can update schemas via Pulsar's representational state transfer (REST) API. A schema has the following properties:

Name

Each schema shares a name with the topic assigned to it.

Payload

The payload is a binary representation of the schema. It is used for retrieving the schema and for schema validation.

Type

Schemas can be primitive types, similar to the following:

---

2 To use an external schema registry, we need to implement the integration. Third-party registries like the AWS Schema Registry and APIcurio have been used in the past.

```
Producer<String> producer = client.newProducer(Schema.STRING).create();
producer.newMessage().value("Surprise!").send();
```

where the schema is defined like this:

```
Schema.TYPE
```

Or they can be complex types defined with key–value pairs or struct. Key–value schemas can be defined like this:

```
Schema<KeyValue<Integer, String>> kvSchema = Schema.KeyValue(
Schema.INT32,
Schema.STRING,
KeyValueEncodingType.SEPARATED
);

Producer<KeyValue<Integer, String>> producer =
    client.newProducer(kvSchema)
    .topic(TOPIC)
    .create();

final int key = 1;
final String value = "Jowanza";

// send the key-value message
producer.newMessage()
.value(new KeyValue<>(key, value))
.send();
```

Structs are common for Avro and Protobuf generation:

```
@Builder
@AllArgsConstructor
@NoArgsConstructor
public static class User {
    String name;
    int age;
}

  Producer<User> producer = client
    .newProducer(Schema.AVRO(User.class))
    .create();
producer
        .newMessage()
        .value(User.builder().name("jowanza")
        .age(26).build()).send();
```

Pulsar primitive types are listed in Table 6-3. An example of a typed producer is shown in Figure 6-8.

User-defined properties

You can set any user-defined property on a Pulsar schema. You can include some notes about the schema or include another link to where the schema is stored in a Git repository.

Table 6-3. Summary of the Primitive Schema Types

Primitive Type	Description
BOOLEAN	True or false (binary value)
INT8	An 8-bit signed integer
INT16	A 16-bit signed integer
INT32	A 32-bit signed integer
INT64	A 64-bit signed integer
FLOAT	A single-precision (32-bit) IEEE 754 floating-point number
DOUBLE	A double-precision (64-bit) IEEE 754 floating-point number
BYTES	A sequence of 8-bit unsigned bytes
STRING	A Unicode character sequence
TIMESTAMP(DATE, TIME)	A logic type representing a specific instant in time with millisecond precision
INSTANT	A single instantaneous point on the timeline with nanosecond precision
LOCAL_DATE	An immutable date-time object that represents a date, often viewed as year-month-day
LOCAL_TIME	An immutable date-time object that represents a time, often viewed as hour-minute-second, with time represented with nanosecond precision
LOCAL_DATE_TIME	An immutable date-time object that represents a date-time, often viewed as year-month-day-hour-minute-second

Figure 6-8. A typed producer. A producer can choose to have a schema attached to a topic and register it with the schema registry.

In addition to client library implementations of schema validation, we can also set schemas from the Pulsar Admin CLI or Pulsar Admin API.

Uploading a schema with the CLI looks like this:

```
$ pulsar-admin schemas upload --filename <schema-definition-file> <topic-name>
```

From the Admin REST API, it looks like this:

```
POST /admin/v2/schemas/:tenant/:namespace/:topic/schema
Body {
    "type": "<schema-type>",
    "schema": "<an-utf8-encoded-string-of-schema-definition-data>",
```

```
        "properties": {} // the properties associated with the schema
    }
```

We can get the latest version of a schema via the CLI with the following command:

```
$ pulsar-admin schemas get <topic-name>

{
    "version": 0,
    "type": "String",
    "timestamp": 0,
    "data": "string",
    "properties": {
        "property1": "string",
        "property2": "string"
    }
}
```

Nonpersistent Topics

Throughout this chapter, we've focused on persistent topics or topics that will persist to Apache ZooKeeper based on lifecycle management. Pulsar also supports nonpersistent topics, which are topics that do not have any persistence in BookKeeper and are simply collected and tailed from the broker.

My focus in this book is on the event streaming offered by Pulsar, so all examples assume a persistent topic. That said, it's worth talking about how it to set up a nonpersistent topic and why we might want to use one.

Use Cases

The only use case for a nonpersistent topic is high throughput and real-time scenarios. In these scenarios, data that arrives to a consumer late has no value to the application; thus, persisting it doesn't have any purpose. You can think of a nonpersistent topic as being like an infinitely running hose: water keeps coming out and consumers need to keep up; and if they are unable to, they need to restart their consumption. In this model, a producer publishes and the consumers (which are subscribed at the time) consume (see Figure 6-9).

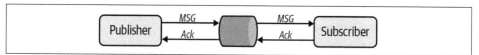

Figure 6-9. In a nonpersistent topic topology, the producer (publisher) sends messages and receives an acknowledgment, and the subscribers (consumers) consume the messages, but only if it is actively consuming.

Nonpersistent topics don't have a "replay" ability, because that would require tracking a cursor and storing data.

Using Nonpersistent Topics

You can use the client libraries, Admin CLI, or Admin API to create nonpersistent topics. For this example, we'll create a nonpersistent topic with the Admin CLI, publish a message with the Pulsar client, and consume the message on the other end. It's important to attach the consumer first because the consumer might not receive the message since it is not persistent.

You can create a nonpersistent topic with the following command:

```
$ pulsar-admin topics create non-persistent://public/default/example-np-topic
```

You can use the Pulsar client CLI to publish a message to the nonpersistent topic:

```
$ bin/pulsar-client produce non-persistent://public/default/example-np-topic \
  --num-produce 1 \
  --messages "Surprise!"
```

Then you can use the Pulsar client CLI to consume the message:

```
$ bin/pulsar-client consume non-persistent://public/default/example-np-topic \
  --num-messages 0 \
  --subscription-name my-ole-sub \
  --subscription-type exclusive
```

Transactions

Transactions are a new feature in Pulsar as of Pulsar 2.7.0. Transactions provide a mechanism for ensuring that all messages are either consumed and committed or rolled back. Transactions are one way to provide the "exactly once" semantics that are coveted by real-time applications. In Pulsar, transactions are implemented as a consumer-process-produce flow (see Figure 6-10) for stream processing. A streaming app consumes messages, processes them, and produces a new flow, all in a single transaction. Either all messages are consumed and processed or none of them are.

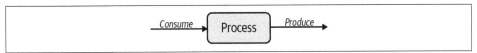

Figure 6-10. In a stream processing flow, messages are consumed from a source, processed, and produced to a new source in a single transaction.

Transactions have two points at which they can fail: either they do not commit in a timely fashion or they are aborted. In either case, messages are rolled back (see Figure 6-11).

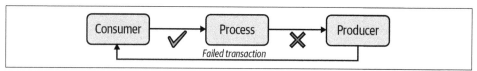

Figure 6-11. If a transaction doesn't commit, all messages are rolled back.

Transactions are enabled through some new consumer and producer APIs. Let's walk through what it looks like for a consumer, for a producer, and then from a consumer to a producer.

A transaction is a new API in Pulsar. You can create a transaction in the Java API:

```
Transaction txn = pulsarClient
        .newTransaction()
        .withTransactionTimeout(1, TimeUnit.MINUTES)
        .build()
        .get();
```

Transactions have a timeout which you can set with any `TimeUnit` API limit. For this example, we're using one minute, which is a long time for a transaction, but it's reasonable for educational purposes.

Now we can use a producer to begin the transaction cycle:

```
producer.newMessage(txn).value("Surprise".getBytes()).send();
```

As part of a `newMessage` we can send a transaction as part of the payload.

From the consumer side, we can confirm or abort the transaction:

```
Message<byte[]> message = consumer.receive();
consumer.acknowledge(message.getMessageId(), txn);
txn.commit().get();
```

In this example, we abort the transaction and it's rolled back:

```
Message<byte[]> message = consumer.receive();
consumer.acknowledge(message.getMessageId(), txn);
txn.abort();
```

While the benefits for client-side applications are there, the stream processing side has an even stronger case for its use.

Pulsar transactions are a new feature in Apache Pulsar as of Pulsar 2.8. They represent a simpler, but more powerful and consistent way forward with *exactly-once semantics*, which means that for a given topology with topics, subscriptions, producers, and consumers, every message is processed once with no chance of duplicate processing. In a stream processing use case, the need for exactly-once processing serves two purposes: it provides guarantees that the system reflects the true state of the world (no duplications) and it reduces any overhead created by processing or storing duplicates of messages.

Summary

In this chapter you learned about the important job that Pulsar producers have in enabling end-to-end stream processing. Among other things, producers are responsible for:

- Determining the schema of a topic
- Compressing data within the topic
- The hashing scheme of a topic
- Chunking messages

Now that you know how producers and consumers work, you're ready to learn about Pulsar IO, a framework for producing and consuming messages from Pulsar.

## CHAPTER 7

Pulsar IO

You've learned about Pulsar's philosophy and architecture, use cases for Pulsar, and the producer and consumer model. Now it's time to work through some examples of using Pulsar. The most accessible place to start on this journey is with Pulsar IO, a framework that lets you easily create, deploy, and manage Pulsar connectors that interact with third-party systems. I'll start by covering the Pulsar IO architecture and then move on to practical examples. At the end of the chapter, we'll write our own Pulsar IO connector.

Pulsar IO Architecture

Before jumping in, I want to justify my reasons for starting with Pulsar IO as the best way to learn about producers and consumers in Pulsar:

- Pulsar IO provides a framework for producing and consuming messages with Apache Pulsar.
- Pulsar IO connectors can work after configuration without additional code by the end user.
- Pulsar IO is simple to understand.

In Chapters 5 and 6, we discussed producers and consumers in Pulsar and how configuration decisions on one side impact the other side. The best way to understand what it takes to write an application that utilizes Pulsar and the implications of configuration decisions is to write an end-to-end application and break down the pieces. Using Pulsar IO, we can use a Pulsar IO connector (or multiple connectors) to achieve our end goal of understanding the message lifecycle and message topologies in Pulsar.

Pulsar has first-party client library support in Java, Python, and Go, and support for languages like Scala and JavaScript through community-supported projects. In Chapter 8, "Pulsar Functions" and Chapter 10, "Pulsar SQL", we'll explore language-specific implementations from the client library side. For now, Pulsar IO gives us everything we need to generate topologies without having to get caught in the specifics of a client library implementation (see Figure 7-1).

Pulsar IO is also simple to understand. That simplicity affords us the time to explore the nuances of Pulsar. With the goals of the chapter laid out, it's time for us to dive in.

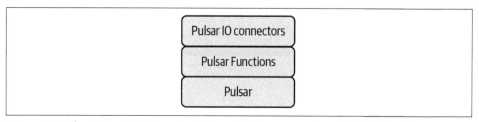

Figure 7-1. The Pulsar IO hierarchy. Pulsar IO is an extension of the Pulsar Functions framework, providing a reusable set of components to build producer and consumer applications on top of Pulsar.

Runtime

Pulsar IO's runtimefoobar consists of Pulsar brokers, Pulsar Functions (covered in depth in Chapter 8), Apache BookKeeper, and the Pulsar IO connector framework. Let's take a look at each component in detail.

Pulsar brokers are a core component of Pulsar. The brokers are the main entry point for all client communication. Brokers also handle message routing and caching in the Pulsar ecosystem. For Pulsar IO, connectors run on brokers by default.

Pulsar Functions are a stream processing runtime that works in conjunction with Pulsar. Pulsar IO runs on top of Pulsar Functions.

Apache BookKeeper is the storage engine for Pulsar and an essential part of Pulsar IO. All configuration is stored and managed in BookKeeper.

The Pulsar IO connector framework is an abstraction on top of Pulsar Functions. It provides the building blocks for writing a Pulsar IO connector, and it makes developers consider aspects of connectors like fault tolerance, serialization, and error handling out of the box (see Figure 7-2).

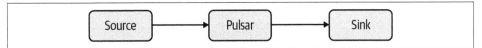

Figure 7-2. An example of the Pulsar IO source–sink model. Sources are applications that are a target for a Pulsar topic. Sinks are destinations for messages stored in Pulsar topics.

Performance Considerations

By default, Pulsar IO topologies utilize compute power, memory, network, and storage from Pulsar brokers. Because Pulsar IO runs on the brokers, the broker resources are the upper bound of Pulsar IO. In practice, Pulsar IO is a purpose-built Pulsar function. In general, functions are lightweight JVM processes; however, resource utilization depends on the volume of messages from a source and the latency characteristics of a sink.

At low message volumes, Pulsar IO with default configurations is unlikely to impact your Pulsar cluster. However, as the number of messages increases, tuning your Pulsar IO configuration becomes a necessity.

Use Cases

Pulsar IO is a general-purpose framework for providing a repeatable, configuration-driven mechanism for moving data to and from Pulsar topics. There is a spectrum of use cases in stream processing, and Pulsar IO is not designed to meet all of them. Pulsar IO's focus is on simplicity and repeatability. It is most appropriate for stream processing tasks with a clear answer for every message that enters the pipeline (see Figure 7-3). Two types of processing jobs with these requirements are simple event processing pipelines and change data capture processes.

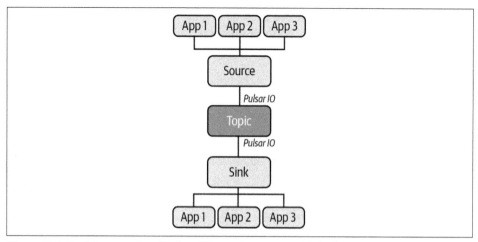

Figure 7-3. In this example of Pulsar IO, applications publish data to a source, such as a database. Pulsar IO consumes data from the source and publishes it to the Pulsar topic. From the topic, a Pulsar IO process moves the data to another system (perhaps another database). Applications then consume the data.

Simple Event Processing Pipelines

Many stream processing jobs have simple requirements. For example, a streaming job might read in all messages from a topic containing user data, remove personally identifiable information, and publish the cleansed data to a new topic. Another example is a topic that contains user phone numbers in different formats; the topic normalizes the data and saves it to a new topic. Both of these stream processing jobs have qualities that make them suitable tasks for Pulsar IO:

- A single source of data (a topic)
- A repeatable process for each message in the topic
- A single destination for each message

Given these qualities, we can write code that handles these events in a repeatable way (see Figure 7-4).

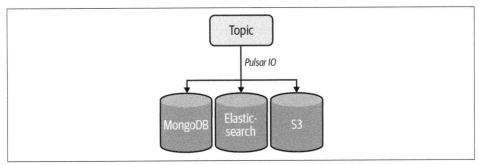

Figure 7-4. In stream processing, a topic sends messages to MongoDB, Elasticsearch, and Amazon S3.

Change Data Capture

Change data capture (CDC) is a pattern used to track changes in a system of record. CDC is commonly utilized in data warehouse technologies for storing transactions from a transactional database. In this architecture, the process that monitors the transaction databases and captures the appropriate changes for the data warehouse is a CDC process. A typical pattern for implementing CDC is the write-ahead log (WAL). Exploring how a WAL works in conjunction with an event system like Apache Pulsar might solidify how Pulsar IO can provide utility.

MySQL is a popular open source database used in hundreds of thousands of applications. MySQL uses a WAL to provide fault tolerance and guarantees around transactions. The WAL has two similarities to an event stream. First, the WAL is a log. We've talked at length about how Pulsar is a distributed log underneath the covers. Second, WALs are an append-only data structure, and the event stream is as well. We can build a repeatable way to move data from a database to a Pulsar topic with these characteristics.

While it is possible to read a WAL and write it directly into a Pulsar topic, this isn't how the built-in CDC implementations work in Pulsar IO. Pulsar IO supports CDC from MySQL, PostgreSQL, MongoDB, Cassandra, Oracle, and Vitess. Pulsar supports CDC for these databases through another open source project called Debezium (see Figure 7-5), an open source CDC server supporting connections to message systems like Apache Kafka, Amazon Kinesis, and Pulsar. Through a connection with Debezium, Pulsar IO can be a CDC mechanism.

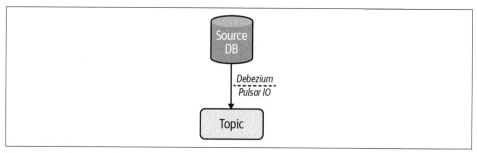

Figure 7-5. Some Pulsar IO connectors utilize Debezium to manage retrieval of data from external systems. In most Pulsar IO implementations, there is a clear separation of responsibilities between Debezium and Pulsar IO.

Considerations

Thus far, we've discussed some of the benefits and concepts of Pulsar IO and focused on its simplicity and use cases. Now let's consider some of the potential pitfalls of using Pulsar IO and what we can do to manage them.

Message Serialization

For source and sink connectors, message serialization is an important consideration when thinking about using Pulsar IO. Message serialization is the process of translating an object from its source type to a format that is acceptable by Pulsar. In Chapter 6, we talked about Pulsar's formats, including strings, Avro, Protobuf, and JSON. Message serialization can show up as an issue in both source and sink connectors; let's explore each.

For a source connector, some message serialization will likely need to occur as data comes from the source and into Pulsar. That serialization can take time and resources to complete, and it can also be prone to error. Database schemas can change, and those changes may not be in lockstep with the Pulsar topic, and thus can lead to failures within the Pulsar IO connector.

Uniform serialization of the source topic in a sink connector is also essential. Maintaining simplicity in a Pulsar IO connector requires that the source data has some uniform shape that can be represented in the configuration for Pulsar IO. Any variability in data shape and type may lead to errors and make Pulsar IO connectors less reliable.

Pipeline Stability

Pulsar IO connectors can incur instability for a few reasons. The source may be unresponsive for source connectors, experience network failures, or be entirely unavailable. Any interruption of this sort may lead to failures in the Pulsar IO connector that require a restart. The same failures can occur for the sink connectors, leading to topics that are full of unacknowledged messages. Most of these failure modes have been considered for the built-in Pulsar IO connectors and have been worked into the connector.

When building your connector, pipeline instability should be top of mind. Following are some questions to consider in the implementation:

- What will happen when my source database isn't able to connect?
- How many times should I try to reconnect after a failed connection?
- How should I handle errors from a source or sink?

This list is not exhaustive, but it provides some context regarding what you should consider when developing a connector and problems you might encounter using a built-in connector.

Failure Handling

Pulsar IO sinks and sources can fail for a variety of reasons, including these:

- Incorrect configuration
- Source or sink becomes unavailable
- Network partitions

If these or any other errors occur in Pulsar IO, the creator of the connector should be able to catch them. In addition, the Pulsar IO framework provides a mechanism for catching connection errors as well as writing errors.

For connection errors, you implement the following interface and throw an exception on failure:

```
/**
 * Open connector with configuration
 *
 * @param config initialization config
 * @param sinkContext
 * @throws Exception IO type exceptions when opening a connector
 */
void open(final Map<String, Object> config,
          SinkContext sinkContext) throws Exception;
```

For writing, there is a similar interface:

```
/**
 * Write a message to Sink
 * @param record record to write to sink
 * @throws Exception
```

```
    */
    void write(Record<T> record) throws Exception;
```

Examples

In this section, we'll work our way through some end-to-end Pulsar IO examples to understand its configuration, the requirements for using it, and what it looks like to write your own Pulsar IO connector (see Figure 7-6). My intent is to illustrate the elegance of Pulsar IO and provide some pointers on how best to utilize it. Note, though, that Pulsar IO is among the least documented aspects of Pulsar as of this writing. The absence of documentation is a reflection of Pulsar IO's simplicity.

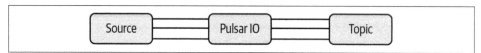

Figure 7-6. In the source–sink architecture, Pulsar IO is the glue that enables the workflow.

Elasticsearch

Elasticsearch is an open source search engine developed by Elastic. Elasticsearch provides developers with an elegant interface for indexing and retrieving data. Search is a critical component of many applications, and indexing stores data suitable for retrieving it with natural language queries. For Pulsar IO, Elasticsearch is a sink connector. This means we configure Pulsar IO to read from a Pulsar topic and write that data to an Elasticsearch index.

Pulsar IO Elasticsearch connectors are built in, meaning the packages needed to use them are already included in the base installation of Apache Pulsar. To use the Elasticsearch connector, we need a Pulsar topic and a handful of configuration values, as shown in Table 7-1.

Table 7-1. Configuration values for use with an Elasticsearch connector

Config Value	Definition
elasticSearchUrl	This is a required field and is the database URL for your Elasticsearch instance.
indexName	The index is a collection in Elasticsearch; this field is required.
typeName	This is the type of data stored in the index.
indexNumberOfShards	Elasticsearch indexes can be sharded; if you can supply this number to Pulsar IO to optimize writes, it is optional.
indexNumberOfReplicas	This is the number of replicas for an index in a clustered deployment of Elasticsearch.
username	This is the username for Elasticsearch.
password	This is the user password for Elasticsearch.

An example configuration for a Pulsar IO Elasticsearch sink connector looks like this:

```
{ "elasticSearchUrl": "http://localhost:9200", "indexName": "my_index",
      "username": "jowanza", "password": "neversharepasswords" }
```

You can run this Elasticsearch connector by saving this configuration file locally, such as in a file called *my_elastic_search.json*, and running it with the Pulsar CLI with the following command:

```
$ bin/pulsar-admin sinks localrun \
    --archive connectors/pulsar-io-elastic-search-2.8.1.nar \
    --tenant public \
    --namespace default \
    --name elasticsearch-test-sink \
    --sink-config my_elastic_search.json \
    --processing-guarantees EFFECTIVELY_ONCE \
    --inputs good_topic
```

Now if we publish the topic good_topic, we will automatically save that result to our Elasticsearch cluster.

Netty

Netty is a server framework for building fast, safe, and reliable network applications. Netty provides some abstractions over network protocols such as HTTP and TCP to enable easier integration with programming languages. For Pulsar IO, the Netty source connector reads data from a specific protocol on a specific port. For HTTP, you can think of it as the Netty server opening a web service specifically for Pulsar. The Netty source connector has a few configuration values:

type
    The network protocol used by Netty (TCP, UDP, or HTTP).

host
    The Netty server hostname.

port
    The port where Pulsar should listen for new messages.

numberOfThreads
    The number of threads the Netty server utilizes for the connection. By default, this value is set to 1, but it may be higher depending on your Netty server.

An example connector looks like this:

```
{ "type": "tcp", "host": "127.0.0.1", "port": "10911", "numberOfThreads": "1" }
```

We can save our config to a file again and call it *netty_config*. From here we can create a Pulsar IO source connector:

```
$ ./bin/pulsar-admin sources localrun \
--archive pulsar-io-2.8.1.nar \
--tenant public \
--namespace default \
--name netty \
--destination-topic-name netty-topic \
--source-config-file netty-source-config.yaml \
--parallelism 1
```

With a running Netty server, we will push traffic from the server to Pulsar IO.

Writing Your Connector

Apache Pulsar supports many connectors out of the box, and those connectors are excellent for the majority of use cases. For bespoke applications, it may be necessary to write your own connector. Fortunately, the Pulsar IO connector framework makes this process simple. In this section, we'll write a Pulsar IO connector for TimescaleDB. This exercise will expose us to the internals of the connector framework and solidify concepts we've discussed so far in this chapter. There is a lot of code that goes into writing a connector, including several files and boilerplate code. For this exercise, I will only talk through the necessary code and will share the code samples in GitHub (*http://www.github.com/josep2*).

TimescaleDB

TimescaleDB is an open source time-series database. TimescaleDB shares some philosophical and performance characteristics with InfluxDB, a database supported out of the box by Pulsar IO. I chose TimescaleDB because there is an adequate amount of documentation on the project, and it provides a relatively easy path forward for a Pulsar IO sink connector. Implementing a sink connector requires only three methods:

open():
  Describes what should happen when the connector starts. In our case, we want to make sure we can reach our TimescaleDB, and if we can't, we want to notify the user immediately.

write():
  Describes how to write the message to the database. In this method, we should handle serialization and work with the interface of TimescaleDB to write the data to it.

close():
  Tells Pulsar what to do when the connector is disconnected or shut down. Ideally, the connector's shutdown should not have harmful effects on Pulsar or the corresponding sink database.

While these are the main methods that we need to implement to create a connector, we have to do a little more to make sure our serialization is correct (from Avro to a format TimescaleDB will accept). We also need to add some logic around how to manage failures.

Here is the open method:

```
public void open(Map<String, Object> config,
    SinkContext sinkContext) throws Exception {

    connectionValues = (Map<String, String>)
      config.getOrDefault("connection", null);

    try {
      timeScaleConnector(connectionValues).connect();

    } catch (Exception e){
      throw new RuntimeException(e);
    }

  }
```

In this method, I try to connect to a TimeScaleDB instance given some connection values in the config. If I am able to connect, then we're good; otherwise, I throw an exception.

Here is the write method:

```
public void write(Record<String> record) throws Exception {
    try {
      timescaleWriter.write(record);
      record.ack();
    } catch (Exception e){
      record.fail();
      throw new RuntimeException(e);
    }
  }
```

In this method, I try to write a record to the timescale writer, and if I am unable to, I throw an exception.

Here is the close method:

```
public void close() throws Exception {
    try {
      timescaleConnectionPool.close();
    } catch (IOException except){
      except.printStackTrace();
    }
  }
```

In this method, I try to close the connection pool, and if I am unsuccessful, I print an error.

Summary

In this chapter you learned about Pulsar IO and the Pulsar IO connector framework. Chapter 8 covers the Pulsar Functions SDK and provides some examples of Pulsar Java and Go functions.

Pulsar Functions

In Chapter 7 I hinted that Pulsar Functions are the bedrock technology used in Pulsar IO. Now we will explore what makes Pulsar Functions unique and why they contribute to make Pulsar an enticing option for an event streaming system.

I've worked with several stream processing engines during my career, from Apache Storm and Spark Streaming to Flink and Kafka Streams. Pulsar Functions are a unique and, perhaps, one of the more agile approaches to the stream processing problem (see Figure 8-1). Pulsar Functions take a problem that requires a large and cumbersome runtime and distill it down to a problem that only requires creating functions that have a topic as an input and a topic as an output. In this chapter you'll learn the reasoning behind Pulsar Functions as a stream processing system. You'll also learn what makes Pulsar Functions unique and what its limitations are. Finally, we'll talk about the deployment models for Pulsar Functions and walk through some use cases.

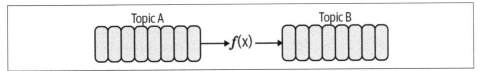

Figure 8-1. Pulsar Functions have a topic as input and a topic as output, and they perform some logic on the data they ingest.

Stream Processing

Organizing and collecting event streams is the first requirement for getting value from real-time data, but enriching, routing, deleting, and triggering actions based on event streams is where the rubber meets the road. Stream processing is the processing of messages in an event stream. At its simplest form, a stream processing system subscribes to an event stream and processes each message according to some user-defined logic. In addition, stream processing systems typically have some requirements around low latency. For example, for some systems, submillisecond latency is required for processing messages that arrive in the event streams storage layer.

In this book, we've explored some of the rich APIs and interaction paradigms Apache Pulsar provides. This list includes Pulsar's approach to schema management, the flexibility of Pulsar's messaging model allowing support of traditional queue architectures and event streaming, and Pulsar's unique publishing topologies. In addition, Pulsar provides an elegant mechanism for storing messages and APIs for varied ways to consume those messages. Finally, Pulsar Functions were born out of a necessity to extend the simplicity of Pulsar to the stream processing world. To appreciate Pulsar's approach to stream processing, it's worth taking a look at some of the systems that tackle stream processing.

But first, let's examine what a stream processing system is. Stream processing systems consume messages from some upstream system, perform some work on the messages, and then do something with the messages afterward. Stream processing systems have a lot of similarities with a plain consumer; we covered this in Chapter 6. However, stream processing systems have one additional requirement: they must understand not only the messages as they consume them but also how the messages relate to one another in time. More concretely, the order of the messages is vital for the system to function and for messages to be processed.

Dealing with message order requires the stream processing system to keep track of the messages and establish timeliness. For example, a stream processing system may say a message is "on time" if it arrives within a 10-second window and is late if it arrives afterward. However, keeping track of the state of messages within a time window is a complex problem and outside the scope of a single consumer. Therefore, stream processing systems like Spark Streaming and Flink are built to manage the complexity of stream processing at scale.

Figure 8-1 illustrates the bare-bones requirements for a distributed stream processing engine like Apache Spark or Flink. These include an orchestration engine, a master-worker architecture, and many times, an additional component for state management. This may seem like a considerable amount of overhead. However, you get a lot in return.

Among other things, you get:

- Performance
- State management guarantees
- Failover
- Checkpointing

- Watermarking

Pulsar Functions, by contrast, were not developed to solve all of these problems in event processing. Instead, Pulsar Functions exist to provide a framework for everyday needs in event processing that can be done using tools already in a Pulsar deployment. Pulsar Functions can also perform out-of-band actions (see Figure 8-2).

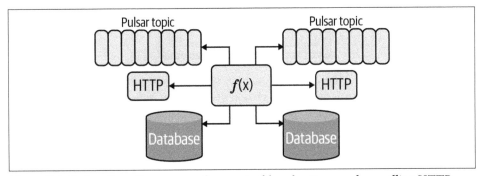

Figure 8-2. Pulsar Functions can perform out-of-band actions such as calling HTTP functions and reaching out to databases, but they ultimately should publish their output to a new topic.

Pulsar Functions Architecture

In the preceding section, we talked about the complexity of modern stream processing systems and why that complexity is necessary. Pulsar Functions do not aim to solve all the use cases of modern, distributed event processing. Instead, Pulsar Functions exist to solve event processing cases, including stateless cases and cases with simple state management needs. With that narrow focus, Pulsar Functions have a simplified runtime and isolation environment. In this section, we'll walk through the Pulsar Functions architecture—specifically, the runtime and the isolation characteristics.

Runtime

Pulsar Functions support three runtime environments:

- Thread-based runtime
- Process-based runtime
- Kubernetes-based runtime

Pulsar Functions can run directly on the Pulsar broker, on separate processes within the Pulsar deployment, or on Kubernetes. In the Pulsar broker, functions can run as a thread or process. Deploying a separate environment for Pulsar Functions to run, the functions have the same options of a thread or process (see Figure 8-3). On Kubernetes, Pulsar Functions run as a separate container. In the next section, we'll walk through the isolation benefits of each of these options.

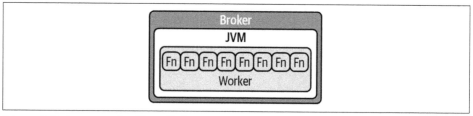

Figure 8-3. An example of how Pulsar Functions operate when run as a process within the broker. The worker runs on the Java virtual machine and handles the lifecycle of each function.

Isolation

Pulsar Functions run in an environment with limited resources. Therefore, the default is the thread-based runtime with a virtual machine shared with other Pulsar Functions. The thread-based runtime is a model that many other stream processing engines use by default. Threads provide adequate isolation, assuming the threading framework is programmed well. However, the thread model does include shared memory with other threads and may have unintended consequences, thereby making it unsuitable for some use cases.

An alternative runtime is a process-based runtime. In this runtime, every Pulsar function spawns its process without shared memory or resources. Pulsar Functions in Go and Python utilize this runtime by default because they cannot run as a JVM thread. While the process-based runtime is more memory safe, you may utilize more resources than you need and require slightly more overhead to manage these use cases (see Figure 8-4).

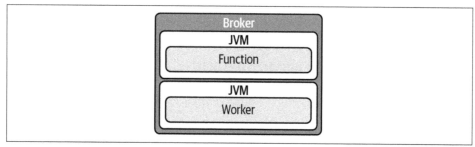

Figure 8-4. An example of functions and workers a JVM environment. In this configuration, the functions are isolated from each other.

The final option for a Pulsar Functions runtime is Kubernetes. The Kubernetes deployment deploys Pulsar Functions as a K8s job with some additional parameters and security configuration (see Figure 8-5). Kubernetes provides isolation in the most meaningful way by deploying functions on separate containers. In addition to isolation, Kubernetes deployments provide a more straightforward path for Pulsar Functions to support more runtimes outside of Java, Go, and Python (see Figure 8-6).

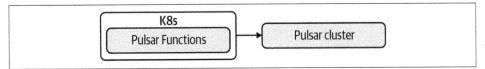

Figure 8-5. Pulsar Functions on Kubernetes (K8s). In this environment, functions are isolated from the Pulsar broker, and Kubernetes manages orchestrating the functions.

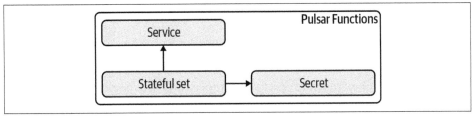

Figure 8-6. When Pulsar Functions run on Kubernetes, the functions run as a stateful set. Functions can be exposed as services and can use secrets for encryption/decryption as well as authentication.

Isolation with Kubernetes Function Deployments

As noted previously, one of the mechanisms for providing isolation in Pulsar Functions is through Kubernetes deployments. Kubernetes deployments of Pulsar Functions move the scheduling from Pulsar to Kubernetes, and utilize the abstractions provided by Kubernetes.

Earlier in this chapter, we talked at length about the simplicity of Pulsar Functions and how an external system is not required to run them. Now we're talking about explicitly using an external system to run them and how that may be better for more complex deployments of Pulsar Functions. Pulsar Functions are one of the selling points of Pulsar to many teams selecting an event streaming solution. However, as teams scale up and usage grows more complex, Pulsar Functions have evolved beyond their intended use case.

The future of Pulsar Functions will be on the broker for simple use cases that are close to the original intent of Pulsar, and Kubernetes deployments will be for complex use cases and topologies.

Use Cases

Now that you understand the Pulsar Functions runtime and execution model, let's explore some code samples and use cases. First, we'll cover how Pulsar Functions are created. The most common use for Pulsar Functions is the simple event processing pipeline, which we'll cover next. It's the most straightforward use case to display the simplicity and elegance of Pulsar Functions. The third and fourth subsections will showcase some of the state management capabilities of Pulsar Functions.

Creating Pulsar Functions

You can create Pulsar Functions in two ways:

- The Admin CLI
- The Admin REST API

Both require either a JAR file (for use with the Java native implementation) or a Go or Python file (for use with those implementations).

To create a new Pulsar function, first you write a class that implements the Pulsar Functions interface:

```
import org.apache.pulsar.functions.api.Context;
import org.apache.pulsar.functions.api.Function;

public class ExclamationFunction implements Function<String, String> {
    @Override
    public String process(String input, Context context) {
        return String.format("%s!", input);
    }
}
```

Then you create the function with the Pulsar Admin CLI:

```
$ bin/pulsar-admin functions create \
  --jar target/my-jar-with-dependencies.jar \
  --classname org.example.functions.ExclamationFunction \
  --tenant public \
  --namespace default \
  --name word-count \
  --inputs persistent://public/default/normal \
  --output persistent://public/default/exclaimed
```

We specified the JAR file with all dependencies (known as a fat Jar), including the class name, tenant, namespace, function name, input topic, and output topic.

Simple Event Processing

Many event processing pipelines require small operations or validations on messages as they arrive in the stream processing system. For example, imagine a battery-powered, internet-connected device that sends its status to a Pulsar topic every few seconds. The status may include:

- The device states (on or off)
- The battery life remaining in the device
- Some location data about where the device is deployed

An event processing application can process new messages as they arrive and send an alert to the owner of devices that have 10% or less battery life left. Let's see what this looks like with Pulsar Functions.

We can create a schema that matches what we've described. But first let's make it an Avro schema:

```
{
    "namespace": "sensordata",
    "type": "record",
    "name": "SensorData",
    "fields":[
        {
            "name": "deviceId",
            "type": {
                "type": "string",
                "logicalType": "uuid"
            }
        },
        {
            "name": "timestamp",
            "type": {
                "type": "long",
                "logicalType": "timestamp-millis"
            }
        },
        {
            "name": "power",
            "type": "int"
        }
    ]
}
```

As we've discussed in this chapter, Pulsar Functions consume messages from a topic and then publish them to a topic after processing. So, for our pipeline, we can move messages on devices that have 10% or less battery life left to a topic for notification and ignore messages on devices that have more than 10% battery life left:

```
package org.example.functions;
import org.apache.pulsar.functions.api.Context;
import org.apache.pulsar.functions.api.Function;

public class SensorData {
    private String deviceId;
    private Long timestamp;
    private int power;

    public SensorData(String deviceId, Long timestamp, int power) {
        this.deviceId = deviceId;
        this.timestamp = timestamp;
        this.power = power;
    }

    // Standard setters and getters
}

public class DeviceChecker implements Function<SensorData, String> {
    @Override
    public String process(SensorData input, Context context) {
        if(input.power < 10){
            return input.deviceId;
        }
    }
}
```

We can run our Pulsar function for checking devices with the following Pulsar CLI commands:

```
$ bin/pulsar-admin functions create \
  --jar target/my-jar-with-dependencies.jar \
  --classname org.example.functions.DeviceChecker \
  --tenant public \
  --namespace default \
  --name device-check \
  --inputs persistent://public/default/devices \
  --output persistent://public/default/almost-dead-devices
```

For event processing pipelines with simple requirements, we can easily use Pulsar Functions to create a robust implementation for them.

Topic Hygiene

Topic hygiene is the process of cleaning up topics after raw ingestion. While data in Pulsar likely has a schema, some aspects of the topic are unusable for the application. Some common examples of raw data that isn't suitable for vast consumption include sensitive data that needs to be scrubbed, topics that need to be translated to a suitable language for the consumer, and topics with a deeply nested schema that benefits from being normalized before consumption. Pulsar Functions are a great framework for performing each of these actions. Each task requires a message-level transformation that can be accomplished in a modern programming language. Let's walk through an example of each.

Sensitivity scrubbing

In this example, we have a topic with employee data. One of the fields contains sensitive data: employees' Social Security numbers (SSNs). In this function, we'll replace the SSN with a string that looks like an SSN:

```
package org.example.functions;
import org.apache.pulsar.functions.api.Context;
import org.apache.pulsar.functions.api.Function;

public class EmployeeRecord {
    private String name;
    private String jobTitle;
    private String ssn;

    public EmployeeRecord(String name, String jobTitle, String ssn) {
        this.name = name;
        this.jobTitle = jobTitle;
        this.ssn = ssn;
    }

    // Standard setters and getters
}

public class EmployeeScrub implements Function<EmployeeRecord, EmployeeRecord> {
    @Override
    public EmployeeRecord process(EmployeeRecord input, Context context) {
        return new EmployeeRecord(input.name, inpt.jobTitle, "xxx-xx-xxxx");
    }
}
}
```

We can also create this function using the Pulsar CLI:

```
$ bin/pulsar-admin functions create \
    --jar target/my-jar-with-dependencies.jar \
    --classname org.example.functions.EmployeeScrub \
    --tenant public \
    --namespace default \
    --name employee-scrub \
    --inputs persistent://public/default/tainted-employees \
    --output persistent://public/default/cleaned-employees
```

Language translation

In this next example, the input topic is a string schema. The string is in English and it's translated into Spanish using a custom class, `org.jowanza.languages .spanish.SpanishTranslator`. The function returns a string in Spanish:

```
package org.example.functions;
import org.apache.pulsar.functions.api.Context;
import org.apache.pulsar.functions.api.Function;
import org.jowanza.languages.spanish.SpanishTranslator;

public class TranslateToSpanish implements Function<String, String> {
    @Override
    public String process(String input, Context context) {
        return SpanishTranslator.translate(input); // Returns a string
    }
}
}
```

We can use the Pulsar Admin API to utilize the function:

```
$ bin/pulsar-admin functions create \
  --jar target/my-jar-with-dependencies.jar \
  --classname org.example.functions.TranslateToSpanish \
  --tenant public \
  --namespace default \
  --name spanish-translator-function \
  --inputs persistent://public/default/english \
  --output persistent://public/default/spanish
```

Schema normalization

For schema normalization, we may have a topic whose data shape isn't ideal, such as an array. We may want to take a value from the array and place it in a new schema:

```
package org.example.functions;
import org.apache.pulsar.functions.api.Context;
import org.apache.pulsar.functions.api.Function;

public class SensorData {
  private String deviceId;
  private int[] hours;

  public SensorData(String deviceId, int[] hours) {
      this.deviceId = deviceId;
      this.hours = hours;
  }

  // Standard setters and getters
}

public class NormalizedSensorData {
  private String deviceId;
  private int recentHour;

  public NormalizedSenorData(String deviceId, int recentHour) {
      this.deviceId = deviceId;
      this.recentHour = recentHour;
  }
```

```
    // Standard setters and getters
  }

  public class DataNormalizer implements Function<SensorData,
    NormalizedSensorData> {
    @Override
    public String process(SensorData input, Context context) {
      return new NormalizedSensorData(input.deviceId, input.hours[0]);
    }
  }
```

We can run this Pulsar function with the CLI:

```
$ bin/pulsar-admin functions create \
  --jar target/my-jar-with-dependencies.jar \
  --classname org.example.functions.DataNormalizer \
  --tenant public \
  --namespace default \
  --name data-normalizer \
  --inputs persistent://public/default/regular \
  --output persistent://public/default/normalized
```

In each of these examples, we provided a small amount of logic and reliably deployed a stream processing job. Pulsar Functions are fully featured and can do more than stateless processing.

Topic Accounting

In this chapter so far, we've focused on stateless stream processing, where previous or past values in the topic don't influence the stream processing engine. For many stream processing cases, being stateless is perfectly adequate; however, keeping some state or reference point is vital. Fortunately, Apache Pulsar is all about storing state, and Pulsar Functions have a built-in mechanism for storing: *state storage*. State storage utilizes Apache BookKeeper to work as a key–value store in conjunction with Pulsar Functions.

One use case for state management is topic accounting, or keeping track of averages, counts, and other metrics in a topic. Pulsar supports a counter for state management as well as a generic state management API. We'll explore both in the following examples.

Incrementing counts

The classic example for incrementing counts is WordCount. Here is a double-word-count function I created that will count each word twice in a given sentence:

```
package org.example.functions;

import org.apache.pulsar.functions.api.Context;
```

```
import org.apache.pulsar.functions.api.Function;

import java.util.Arrays;

public class DoubleWordCountFunction implements Function<String, Void> {
    @Override
    public Void process(String input, Context context) throws Exception {
        Arrays.asList(input.split(" ")).forEach(word -> {
            String counterKey = word.toLowerCase();
            context.incrCounter(counterKey, 2);
        });
        return null;
    }
}
```

Getting and setting state

I can set state in my functions by using a method defined on the Context object:

```
public class DataSetter implements Function<String, Void>{
  public void process (String input, Context context){
    context.setState("jowanza", "good guy".getBytes());
    return null;
  }

}
```

I can also retrieve state in a function by using the Context object:

```
public class DataGetter implements Function<String, Void>{
  public void process (String input, Context context){
    context.getState("jowanza"); // Byte Array of "good guy string"
    return null;
  }

}
```

Summary

In this chapter we covered Pulsar Functions in depth. We started with the architecture, covered some runtime considerations, and then worked through some detailed examples of how to use Pulsar Functions. Now we'll take a small break from methods of accessing Pulsar topics and talk about storage extensions for Pulsar. Understanding storage extensions will help us better understand Pulsar SQL.

## CHAPTER 9

Tiered Storage

Pulsar has immutable storage as a primitive and interfaces for interacting with that storage via client libraries, Pulsar Functions, and Pulsar IO. This means we can do things like replay topic data from the beginning (or at a specific offset) as well as handle events like consumers going offline for periods of time. Supporting high-performance writing and retrieval of data in Pulsar requires the bookies in a Pulsar cluster to utilize disk technology, which is expensive relative to alternatives. In Chapter 5, you learned how Pulsar operators can ensure that data is deleted when it's no longer used. What if we want to keep the data indefinitely but store it in a more cost-effective way?

Pulsar tiered storage is a mechanism for offloading data that doesn't have immediate value on BookKeeper to a cheaper and more flexible storage solution (see Figure 9-1).

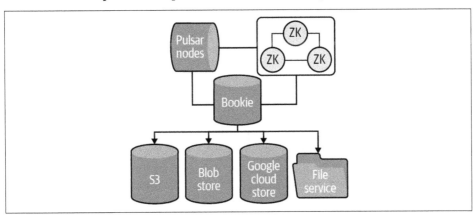

Figure 9-1. In Pulsar's tiered storage ecosystem, data moves from bookies to other services like object storage or distributed file storage for long-term data storage needs.

In this chapter we'll cover some of the motivation for tiered storage and discuss how to set up tiered storage using Pulsar Admin APIs and the console.

Storing Data in the Cloud

In the world of data storage, not all mechanisms of storing data are considered equal. Each approach to storing data is a trade-off between cost, efficiency, and fault tolerance. Since Pulsar is a cloud-native technology, we'll focus on the following three cloud mechanisms for storing data:

- File
- Block
- Object

Table 9-1 provides a summary of common ways these three data storage mechanisms are used in the cloud.

Table 9-1. Summary of cloud-based storage solutions

Storage mechanism	Cost	Reliability	Use cases
File	$$	Great reliability in cloud settings.	Network attached storage.
Block	$$$	Great reliability in cloud settings.	Cloud server storage (hot).
Object	$	Cloud applications are impeccable, reliable, and durable.	Cold storage/big data storage.

The most common type of storage for a BookKeeper cluster is block storage. Popular public cloud providers like Amazon Web Services and Azure Cloud typically bundle block storage with their server offerings. Block storage is the most expensive of the three types, but it provides an easy way to scale up when needed for the cloud environment. As we consider a Pulsar cluster, when the storage needs of the cluster grow, we will encounter more costs in terms of servers and block storage (see Figure 9-2).

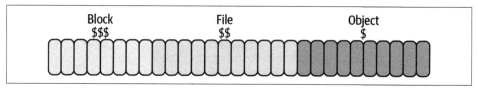

Figure 9-2. Pricing tiers. Block storage (typically what's found for a cloud application) is the most expensive because it has performance requirements for quick writing and reading. File storage is cheaper as it has fewer requirements than block storage. Object storage is even cheaper and is suitable for long-term storage.

It would be ideal if, as our needs changed in the cloud, we could move our data to a cheaper storage solution. As our application matures, we may have different needs to meet in our Pulsar cluster. For example, we may keep higher performance data for our clusters on block storage and, as the data becomes stale, we move it to file (the file system on your laptop) or block storage (see Figures 9-3 and 9-6).

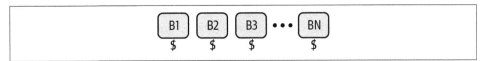

Figure 9-3. BookKeeper allows for a scale-out architecture, but as we add more nodes to our cluster, the costs associated with the server and storage also grow.

What we need is a way to reserve precious cluster resources (block storage) and move old data from Pulsar to another system. Pulsar tiered storage provides a way to move data from BookKeeper (where data is stored in Pulsar) to other storage mechanisms, including object storage and file storage.

While the file storage option for offloading data in Pulsar is interesting, we're going to focus on object storage because object storage is intentionally built to store data of many types and has APIs for solving a wide range of problems. It's worth taking a moment to dive into some of the solutions object stores provide in the wider data ecosystem.

Object Storage

Object storage is not a new concept, having originated in the early 1990s.[1] Object stores have a different paradigm from file storage in that an object is composed of:

- Data (the actual bytes that need to be stored)
- Metadata (arbitrary values about the object)
- Permissions (who can access the object)
- An ID (a unique identifier for the object)

Instead of being stored in a hierarchical filesystem, objects are stored in what are called buckets (see Figure 9-4).

1 M. Factor, K. Meth, D. Naor, O. Rodeh, and J. Satran, "Object storage: The future building block for storage systems," in *2005 IEEE International Symposium on Mass Storage Systems and Technology* (New York: IEEE, 2005): 119–123, doi: 10.1109/LGDI.2005.1612479.

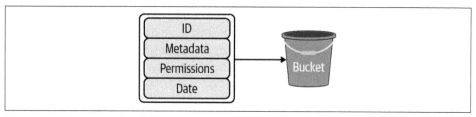

Figure 9-4. An example of object storage. Objects combine metadata, data, permissions, and an identifier that are stored in a bucket.

A bucket is a fully qualified namespace within the storage system. Object stores allow for a scalable solution for storing data redundancy. However, since object stores are not a filesystem, they are accessed through different APIs. Object stores have semantics such as the following (see Figure 9-5):

GET
    Retrieve an object by ID.

PUT
    Place a name object with an ID in a bucket.

LIST
    List all objects in a bucket.

DELETE
    Delete an object by ID.

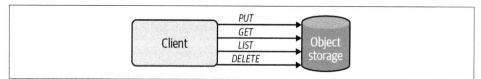

Figure 9-5. Object storage clients perform PUT, GET, LIST, and DELETE on objects within a bucket.

For most consumer use, object stores did not make sense. Consumers were used to filesystems that had some similarities to object stores but were limited in different ways that we won't get into for this discussion. In the early 2000s, the internet began to attract different types of users and applications, and object stores became relevant. Today object stores are a critical component in public cloud usage. Object storage on the public cloud offers essentially unlimited storage for minimal costs (see Table 9-2).

Table 9-2. Summary of object storage offerings on the public cloud

Public cloud provider	Object storage offering	Cost per GB of storage[a]
Amazon Web Services	S3	$0.023 per GB per month
Google Cloud Platform	Cloud Storage	$0.020 per GB per month
Azure Cloud	Blob Store	$0.018 per GB per month
IBM Cloud	Cloud Object Storage	$0.0144 per GB per month
Oracle Cloud	Oracle Object Storage	$0.0255 per GB per month

[a] Prices as of October 2021. There are several caveats to this pricing, including bulk discounts.

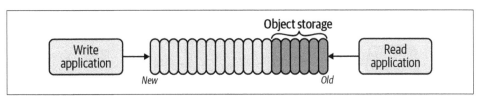

Figure 9-6. An example of how Pulsar tiered storage works. Most of the value can be found in the newest data as it is being written to Pulsar. As data gets older, moving it to object storage becomes more economical.

In Chapter 4, we talked a bit about how BookKeeper can be used as an object store for some projects. BookKeeper ledgers have some similar properties to objects in an object store. Table 9-3 summarizes their similarities and differences.

Table 9-3. A comparison of objects stored in object storage and data stored in BookKeeper ledgers

	Object store	BookKeeper ledger
Data (bytes)	Object stores store bytes of data.	Ledgers store bytes of data.
Metadata	Metadata is required for objects.	Metadata is required for most use cases.
Permissions	Permissions are explicitly required.	Permissions are not required but can be implemented.
Unique ID	Every object has a unique ID.	Every ledger has a unique ID.

With an immutable ledger, knowing when to move data is easy to determine, and since object storage can store arbitrarily large objects (and arbitrarily many), it's also a good destination for our offloading. Now we can ask the question, what else do we get out of storing data in object storage?

Use Cases

In addition to offloading data from a Pulsar cluster for cost reasons, there are other reasons for adopting tiered storage, including the following:

- Out-of-band replication
- Adopting an event sourcing model for your application
- Managing disaster recovery scenarios

Replication

Replication is the process of keeping data synchronized. The canonical example of replication in software systems is replicating from a transaction database to a data warehouse. By definition, Pulsar's tiered storage is a replication mechanism. It replicates data from a source to an offloaded storage engine (see Figure 9-7).

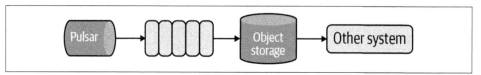

Figure 9-7. Pulsar tiered storage can be used to replicate data from Pulsar to object storage, where it can be used in another system.

Pulsar's tiered storage doesn't replicate data in real time; it replicates it based on configuration. From an end-user perspective, we tell Pulsar at what age data is considered "old," or how large the ledger should be before data should be offloaded to the object store. Thinking of tiered storage as a replication technique has some powerful implications. For example, we can build applications that utilize object storage which can scale to multiple clients, instead of using Pulsar for that purpose.

CQRS

Most of the applications we use provide a way for us to create, edit, view, and delete things. For a concrete example, think about your favorite photo sharing application. You can add new pictures to the service, edit your pictures and descriptions, view your photos and photos of other users in the service, and delete your photos if you desire. Of course, each of these interactions requires some interaction with permanent storage in a database or an event streaming platform like Pulsar.

If we examine the needs of an application tasked with creating new entries, viewing entries, editing entries, and deleting them, there may be some differences in how we might handle these concerns from a development angle. When you open the photo application to share a photo, any perceived latency or failure to post the photo could be detrimental to your usage. Instead, the application developers might consider a fast and reliable path for saving new pictures, like a Pulsar client writing messages to the broker.

When viewing other users' pictures, the experience may not need to be updated in real time and may be better read from an offloaded source, such as directly from the object storage. Utilizing one path for writing data and an utterly different path for reading data is the command query responsibility segregation (CQRS) pattern (see Figure 9-8).

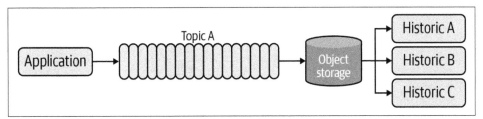

Figure 9-8. In this example of the Command Query Responsibility Segregation pattern, the application writes data to Topic A; as the data reaches a certain maturity, is it offloaded to object storage. From there, applications that are responsible for retrieving data can retrieve it from the object store rather than the messaging system.

In this example, we can keep all our new photos on a fresh stream in a topic. When photos get older, we can offload them to object storage. If a user wants to retrieve an old photo, it is retrieved from object storage.

Disaster Recovery

Apache Pulsar clusters run on the internet and have many moving parts. While each component of Pulsar is measurably reliable independently, none of the components can withstand the complete disaster of a public cloud provider's infrastructure or disasters that may occur in an on-premises environment. One defense against this is to create more redundancy in the system. Tiered storage provides a way to offload data from a reliable system (BookKeeper) to an even more reliable system (an object store); see Figure 9-9.

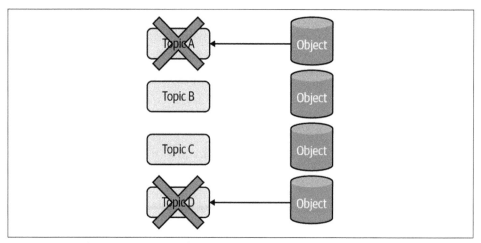

Figure 9-9. In disaster scenarios where Pulsar data is destroyed, having offloaded data can help speed system recovery.

As an example, let's consider Amazon S3, perhaps the most popular object storage platform in the world. Amazon states (*https://oreil.ly/qZkyJ*) that S3 has 11 nines (99.999999999) of reliability for any object stored on S3. We've talked about Book-Keeper and the reliability of the data stored there. As operators of BookKeeper, we increase our quorum sizes to deal with potential disasters, or even come up with a multiple-availability-zone solution. That said, having an additional level of redundancy offloaded from ledgers only helps the recovery scenario.

Offloading Data

Let's take a look at how offloading data from Pulsar bookies to object storage works. In the following subsections, we'll discuss the schema and columnar offloader in Pulsar and how we can configure our namespace for offloading.

Pulsar Offloaders

Apache Pulsar uses Apache jClouds for its implementation of tiered storage for object storage. Apache jClouds is an open source library that brings cloud-native functionality to Java. The concept of offloaders is simply a set of configurations and rules for how to offload and where to offload the data (see Figure 9-10).

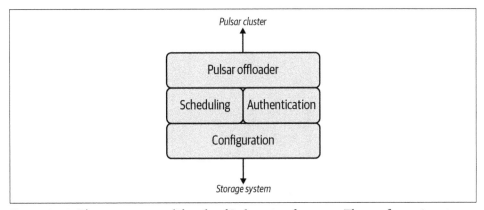

Figure 9-10. The management lifecycle of Pulsar tiered storage. The configurations to external systems and authentication, scheduling, and unloading mechanisms are stored as metadata and executed when required.

For object storage, Pulsar supports Amazon S3 as well as Google Cloud Storage. We'll cover each in this section. For each object store we won't cover creating a bucket; good tutorials for how to do that are available online, and I will share some of the tutorials I find helpful in the footnotes.

Amazon S3

To set up object storage on Amazon S3, follow these steps:

- Create an S3 bucket (*https://oreil.ly/QFJPr*).
- Ensure that your AWS credentials are accessible via the CLI.
- Edit the *conf/pulsar_env.sh* file to include AWS credentials and role ARNs, as listed in the following code snippet:

```
export AWS_ACCESS_KEY_ID=<id> // AN AWS ACCESS Key
export AWS_SECRET_ACCESS_KEY=<Key> // AN AWS ACCESS KEY SECRET
PULSAR_EXTRA_OPTS="${PULSAR_EXTRA_OPTS} ${PULSAR_MEM} ${PULSAR_GC}
-Daws.accessKeyId=<id> -Daws.secretKey=<key>
-Dio.netty.leakDetectionLevel=disabled
-Dio.netty.recycler.maxCapacity.default=1000
-Dio.netty.recycler.linkCapacity=1024"
s3ManagedLedgerOffloadRole=<aws role arn for your role> // The Role ARN
s3ManagedLedgerOffloadRoleSessionName=session-name // A Session name
```

- Edit your *broker.conf* file using the values in Table 9-4.
- Start the broker.

Table 9-4. Broker values for the managed ledger offloader for AWS S3

Configuration value	Description	Required	Default value/examples
`managedLedgerOffloadDriver`	Offloader driver name, which is case insensitive	Yes	`aws-s3`
`offloadersDirectory`	Offloader directory	Yes	`offloaders`
`s3ManagedLedgerOffloadBucket`	Bucket	Yes	`pulsar-topic-offload`
`s3ManagedLedgerOffloadRegion`	Bucket region	No	`eu-west-3`
`s3ManagedLedgerOffloadServiceEndpoint`	`s3ManagedLedgerOffloadServiceEndpoint=https://s3.YOUR_REGION.amazonaws.com`	Only if Region is set	NA
`s3ManagedLedgerOffloadReadBufferSizeInBytes`	Size of read block	No	1 MB
`s3ManagedLedgerOffloadMaxBlockSizeInBytes`	Size of write block	No	64 MB
`managedLedgerMinLedgerRolloverTimeMinutes`	Minimum time in minutes between ledger rollover for a topic	No	2
`managedLedgerMaxEntriesPerLedger`	Maximum number of entries to append to a ledger before triggering a rollover	No	500
`s3ManagedLedgerOffloadReadBufferSizeInBytes`	Block size for each individual read when reading back data from AWS S3	No	1 MB
`s3ManagedLedgerOffloadMaxBlockSizeInBytes`	Maximum size of a "part" sent during a multipart upload to AWS S3 (cannot be smaller than 5 MB)	No	64 MB

In the preceding steps, the configuration is set for all topics across all namespaces. You can override this and set an offload policy with the Pulsar CLI:

```
bin/pulsar-admin namespaces set-offload-threshold --size 15M tenant-a/namespace-a
```

You can also do this with the Pulsar Admin API (see Table 9-4 for the appropriate values):

```
POST /https://pulsar.apache.org/admin/v2/namespaces/
        {tenant}/{namespace}/offloadPolicies
Body
{
  "offloadersDirectory": "string",
  "managedLedgerOffloadDriver": "string",
  "managedLedgerOffloadMaxThreads": 0,
  "managedLedgerOffloadPrefetchRounds": 0,
  "managedLedgerOffloadThresholdInBytes": 0,
  "managedLedgerOffloadDeletionLagInMillis": 0,
  "managedLedgerOffloadedReadPriority": "BOOKKEEPER_FIRST",
  "s3ManagedLedgerOffloadRegion": "string",
  "s3ManagedLedgerOffloadBucket": "string",
  "s3ManagedLedgerOffloadServiceEndpoint": "string",
  "s3ManagedLedgerOffloadMaxBlockSizeInBytes": 0,
  "s3ManagedLedgerOffloadReadBufferSizeInBytes": 0,
  "s3ManagedLedgerOffloadCredentialId": "string",
  "s3ManagedLedgerOffloadCredentialSecret": "string",
  "s3ManagedLedgerOffloadRole": "string",
  "s3ManagedLedgerOffloadRoleSessionName": "string",
  "managedLedgerOffloadBucket": "string",
  "managedLedgerOffloadRegion": "string",
  "managedLedgerOffloadServiceEndpoint": "string",
  "managedLedgerOffloadMaxBlockSizeInBytes": 0,
  "managedLedgerOffloadReadBufferSizeInBytes": 0,
  "s3Driver": true
}
```

You can also run a manually triggered offload with the following Pulsar CLI command:

```
bin/pulsar-admin topics offload --size-threshold 15M tenant-a/my-namespace/topicABC
```

Here's a complete example of settings within a *broker.conf* file for AWS:

```
managedLedgerOffloadDriver=aws-s3
offloadersDirectory=offloaders
s3ManagedLedgerOffloadRegion=us-west-2
s3ManagedLedgerOffloadServiceEndpoint=https://s3.us-west-2.amazonaws.com
```

Google Cloud Storage

To set up object storage on Google Cloud Storage, follow these steps:

- Create a bucket (*https://oreil.ly/W6T2o*) in Google Cloud Storage.
- Create a service account (*https://oreil.ly/aMz7o*).
- Edit your *broker.conf* file with the values shown in Table 9-5.
- Start the broker.

A service account is a way to enable API access to Google Cloud products. When access is enabled, the user can get an authentication key from Google to allow other products to use the Google Cloud service via a Google Cloud API. In our case, we want to create a service account for OAuth access to Google Cloud. I've linked to some documentation from Google (*https://oreil.ly/yKsUf*) on how to set this up.

We need to place the keyfile somewhere on the broker in order to allow Pulsar to authenticate with Google Cloud. A keyfile looks something like this:

```
{
  "type": "service_account",
  "project_id": "project-id",
  "private_key_id": "key-id",
  "private_key":
    "-----BEGIN PRIVATE KEY-----\nprivate-key\n-----END PRIVATE KEY-----\n",
  "client_email": "service-account-email",
  "client_id": "client-id",
  "auth_uri": "https://accounts.google.com/o/oauth2/auth",
  "token_uri": "https://accounts.google.com/o/oauth2/token",
  "auth_provider_x509_cert_url": "https://www.googleapis.com/oauth2/v1/certs",
  "client_x509_cert_url":
    https://www.googleapis.com/robot/v1/metadata/x509/service-account-email
}
```

Once we have the keyfile and place it in our Pulsar broker, we edit our *broker.conf* to include the location to that keyfile:

```
gcsManagedLedgerOffloadServiceAccountKeyFile="data/myproj.json"
```

Table 9-5. Values for broker configuration with Google Cloud Storage

Configuration value	Description	Required	Default/Example
`managedLedgerOffloadDriver`	Offloader driver name	Yes	`google-cloud-storage`
`offloadersDirectory`	Offloader directory	Yes	`offloaders`
`gcsManagedLedgerOffloadBucket`	Bucket	Yes	`pulsar-topic-offload`
`gcsManagedLedgerOffloadRegion`	Bucket region	Yes	`us-a-2`
`gcsManagedLedgerOffloadServiceAccount KeyFile`	Authentication	Yes	`Users/user-name/Downloads/ project-804d5e6a6f33.json`
`gcsManagedLedgerOffloadReadBuffer SizeInBytes`	Size of block read	No	NA
`gcsManagedLedgerOffloadMaxBlockSizeIn Bytes`	Size of block write	No	NA
`managedLedgerMinLedgerRolloverTime Minutes`	Minimum time between ledger rollover for a topic	No	NA
`managedLedgerMaxEntriesPerLedger`	The maximum number of entries to append to a ledger before triggering a rollover	No	5,000
`gcsManagedLedgerOffloadReadBuffer SizeInBytes`	Block size for each individual read when reading back data from GCS	No	1 MB
`gcsManagedLedgerOffloadMaxBlockSizeIn Bytes`	Maximum size of a "part" sent during a multipart upload to GCS	No	64 MB

In the preceding steps, the configuration is set for all topics across all namespaces. You can override this and set an offload policy with the Pulsar CLI:

```
bin/pulsar-admin namespaces set-offload-threshold --size 15M tenant-a/namespace-a
```

Or the Pulsar Admin API:

```
POST /https://pulsar.apache.org/admin/v2/namespaces/{tenant}/{namespace}/offloadPolicies
Body
{
  "offloadersDirectory": "string",
  "managedLedgerOffloadDriver": "string",
  "managedLedgerOffloadMaxThreads": 0,
  "managedLedgerOffloadPrefetchRounds": 0,
  "managedLedgerOffloadThresholdInBytes": 0,
  "managedLedgerOffloadDeletionLagInMillis": 0,
  "managedLedgerOffloadedReadPriority": "BOOKKEEPER_FIRST",
  "gcsManagedLedgerOffloadRegion": "string",
  "gcsManagedLedgerOffloadBucket": "string",
  "gcsManagedLedgerOffloadMaxBlockSizeInBytes": 0,
  "gcsManagedLedgerOffloadReadBufferSizeInBytes": 0,
  "gcsManagedLedgerOffloadServiceAccountKeyFile": "string",
  "managedLedgerOffloadBucket": "string",
  "managedLedgerOffloadRegion": "string",
  "managedLedgerOffloadServiceEndpoint": "string",
  "managedLedgerOffloadMaxBlockSizeInBytes": 0,
  "managedLedgerOffloadReadBufferSizeInBytes": 0,
  "gcsDriver": true
}
```

You can also run a manually triggered offload with the following Pulsar CLI command:

```
bin/pulsar-admin topics offload --size-threshold 15M tenant-a/my-namespace/topicABC
```

Here is a complete example of settings within a *broker.conf* file for GCP:

```
managedLedgerOffloadDriver=google-cloud-storage
offloadersDirectory=offloaders
gcsManagedLedgerOffloadBucket=my-offload-bucket
gcsManagedLedgerOffloadServiceAccountKeyFile=/my/file/path/key.json
```

Earlier in this chapter we talked about other cloud storage platforms such as Azure Blob Storage and IBM Object Storage. Pulsar can support these platforms in two ways. If they have an S3-compatible API, you can use the same S3 configurations we discussed. If not, it's a matter of allowing Apache jClouds to support them and then making some changes to Pulsar to allow them as well.

Retrieving Offloaded Data

Now that you know how to move data off the Apache BookKeeper tier and into a more cost-efficient storage mechanism, and the advantages of doing so, let's focus on how to get offloaded data back into Pulsar.

Offloaded data are objects written to the file or object storage. There are three ways to interact with offloaded data:

- Directly through the object store
- Repopulating the topic with offloaded data
- Utilizing the Pulsar client

Interacting with Object Store Data

Earlier in this chapter, we talked about the CQRS pattern and why, for some applications utilizing this pattern, we might want to store data using Pulsar clients and retrieve it using an object store (see Figure 9-11).

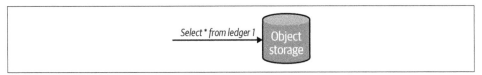

Figure 9-11. An example of how a SQL engine could be used to retrieve BookKeeper segments from object storage. The SQL engine would need to be able to parse BookKeeper files.

It's worth reiterating that this approach has some limitations. First, data that is offloaded from BookKeeper to object storage is not necessarily human readable or in common machine-readable formats like CSV, Parquet, or JSON. It's possible to build a parser to allow for a SQL interface over the journal files, but one does not exist off the shelf.

Repopulating Topics

Pulsar clients can automatically read offloaded data (we will discuss this in the next subsection). However, there are some reasons why you may not want to enable the ability to read from offloaded data automatically and may want fine-grained control over which data a consumer can retrieve. In these cases, instead of automatically reading from offloaded topics, we may load data on a new topic and point the consumer to that topic for older data (see Figure 9-12).

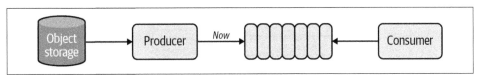

Figure 9-12. A producer can retrieve data from BookKeeper and create a new topic for consumers with special permission to consume the data.

This pattern may seem cumbersome and error prone on the surface, and while it can be, there are some excellent reasons to adopt it. For example, some companies, such as those in the financial and medical arenas, must keep records for up to 10 years. As a result, there is some risk to allow ingestion of old records, and an organization may decide to disable retrieval of old records. A procedure that restores retrieved data into a new topic for audit could be safer.

For this use case, you can use an object storage client library to read data from the bucket, parse the ledger into messages, and then write the messages out to Pulsar. This is a nontrivial amount of work, but it is doable if you have a specific use case. An alternative would be to build a Pulsar IO connector that had an object store source connector, and then parse the ledgers stored in S3 and write them to a Pulsar topic.

Utilizing Pulsar Client

Pulsar topics and the location where cursor data is tracked are stored in the managed ledger. The managed ledger tells the Pulsar broker not only which ledger to retrieve for a consumer, but also where that ledger is stored (see Figure 9-13). As a consumer, it's not necessary to worry about where the data is stored; the Pulsar broker will retrieve the data as needed from wherever it may be (see Figure 9-14). This is the easiest way to interact with offloaded data in Pulsar, and it provides a transparent way for the consumer to get the data it needs.

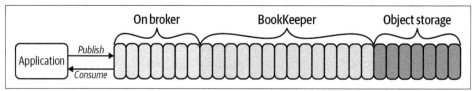

Figure 9-13. Pulsar brokers use the managed ledger cache to work as a tail log. Book-Keeper is where data is stored when it's required for the Pulsar cluster. Object storage (tiered storage) is where any long-lived data should go.

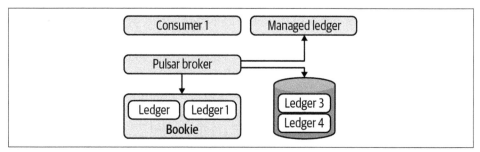

Figure 9-14. When consuming data, the Pulsar broker interacts with ZooKeeper and the managed ledger tells the broker where data is stored. It can retrieve data from Book-Keeper or from object storage. Either way is transparent to the consumer.

For an implementation, suppose the earliest offsets in a Pulsar topic are offloaded and newer data is still stored in BookKeeper. We simply need to start our consuming at the earliest offset, and the Pulsar broker will handle retrieving data from the offloaded space:

```
import org.apache.pulsar.client.api.MessageId;
import org.apache.pulsar.client.api.Reader;

Reader<byte[]> reader = pulsarClient.newReader()
    .topic("read-from-topic")
    .startMessageId(MessageId.earliest) // get data at earliest offset
    .create();

while (true) {
    Message message = reader.readNext();

    // Get messages after this point
}
```

Summary

In this chapter you learned about Apache Pulsar tiered storage. Specifically, you learned how it's more than a cost-savings mechanism; it's also a mechanism to enable new types of interactions with Apache Pulsar. You also learned that the way Pulsar stores data in BookKeeper creates a sensible link between an object store and Pulsar. Now we'll move on to learning how to query Pulsar topics with the SQL language.

## CHAPTER 10

Pulsar SQL

At this point, we know we can interact with Pulsar in the following ways:

- Pulsar CLI
- Pulsar Admin API
- Pulsar clients
- Pulsar Functions
- Pulsar IO

Another way we can interact with Pulsar topics is through Structured Query Language (SQL). With Pulsar SQL, we can treat topics as tables and query them with SQL. However, before diving into how querying topics with SQL is possible, we should ask why do this at all? After all, using another tool or another language has some disadvantages that we should consider as well. Among these disadvantages are:

- Increased complexity from managing more semantics
- Cost considerations
- Cognitive overhead from managing new tools

We know Apache Pulsar is a storage system for event streams. With that lens, we can see the necessity and utility of alternative data interaction mechanisms. For example, with Pulsar Functions, we get a simple API that allows us to manipulate messages one at a time. With Pulsar IO, we get a repeatable mechanism for moving data to and from Pulsar topics. What advantage does querying a topic with SQL bring to the table?

SQL is the most ubiquitous programming language. Analytics engineers, designers, programmers, data scientists, and executives can all utilize it. In addition, popular databases like PostgreSQL, MySQL, Oracle, and Redshift all use a dialect of SQL to query data. Pulsar topics contain event data and are often the ingress point for an application. Enabling more people to access the data at this point in the pipeline can unlock new insights and new applications, and potentially detect problems early in the pipeline.

While querying a topic with SQL may sound convenient, the abstraction is much more potent than that. By understanding the interchange between streams and tables, we can use streams when appropriate and tables when appropriate. Or we can *have our cake and eat it too*. This chapter will dive deeper into this idea of streams and tables and extend our understanding of how these abstractions can enhance our architectures. It will end by walking through using Pulsar SQL to solve some real-world problems.

Streams as Tables

Many modern applications require the storage, manipulation, and retrieval of data. A canonical example of an application with these requirements is a to-do list. The to-do list needs to store, edit, and retrieve all of your tasks. How should the current state of the list be represented? In an event stream model, we may create a topic for the list. Each time we make a change to the list, we publish data to that stream. On the consumer end of the application, the client can subscribe to the same topic and update the list as dictated by the topic. In addition to updating the state based on the last message in the topic, we can also re-create any state in the past by replaying the topic from the start (see Figure 10-1).

An alternative to this event stream is the table or database way of collecting the data. In this model, every time a change is made to the to-do list, we can either create a new row in the table or edit an existing row. We can always retrieve the current state of affairs and edit that state in this paradigm, but we cannot reconstruct all previous states from the current table (see Figure 10-2).[1]

Is there anything inherently better about the table paradigm than the stream paradigm? No. Each paradigm exposes a level of granularity that is appropriate for the problem. If you consider the differences between the two in more detail, you may realize the relationship between them.

To make the duality of streams and tables a little more apparent, let's explore an example. Imagine building a score tracker for a basketball game. As the game is in

---

1 In a table model, you can create tables that are "history" tables which keep track of all the changes in a stream.

play, many events can occur. Players can score points, commit turnovers, steal the basketball, and block shots, among other activities (see Figure 10-1).

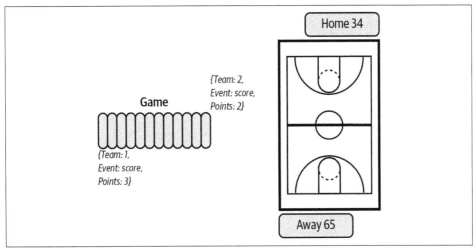

Figure 10-1. A basketball game as an event stream. As each team has an event (scores points), a new entry is added to the topic.

For our purposes, we'll focus on the task of keeping track of the score. We can model the score as an event with the following schema:

```
{ "team" : <team_id>,
"event": "score",
"points": <number>}
```

Each time the score increases, our application can publish a message with the team and the incremental score value. At any point, we can calculate the score by summing all of the score events that have taken place from the beginning of the topic until this moment. If we know the score now, we can append the new event to the existing score. Whenever we sum the complete history of that topic, we are creating a table view. We represent our score as what it is at this exact moment. When we append updates to a stream of scores, that is the event stream model. To summarize, aggregating actions on a stream allows us to represent that stream as a table.

Focusing on this point a little more, there is an interchangeability between streams and tables. A properly represented and designed event system can be represented as a table. Consider Figure 10-2, which shows a stream of orders with IDs, amounts, and timestamps. We can explore a few ways in which we can go from the stream of orders to table views and summaries.

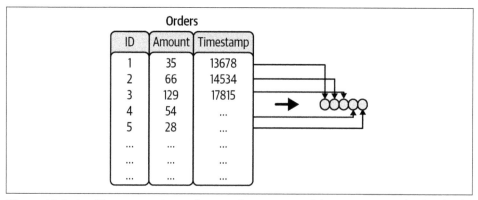

Figure 10-2. A table representing orders can be constructed from a stream of individual orders.

Suppose we have an orders topic with the following schema:

```
{ "id": <int>,
"amount": <double>
"timestamp": <long>
}
```

Now suppose we want to summarize all sales for the past 24 hours in the stream. We could express this with SQL that looks something like this:

```
Select sum(amount) from orders where time_stamp_function(timestamp, 24h);
```

Further, if we want to get sales for a specific ID, we can make some more adjustments to our query:

```
Select sum(amount) from orders where time_stamp_function(timestamp, 24h) and id=1;
```

Additionally, we can find all sales in the past 24 hours that were over $100:

```
Select id, amount from orders where time_stamp_function(timestamp, 24h) and amount > 100;
```

Going from a stream to a table gives us a new way to express stream processing and has some immediate real-world value. One question that warrants further investigation is, what does it mean to have a table that is unbounded? To answer that question, we need to better understand the history of querying data and querying streams of data.

SQL-on-Anything Engines

In the 2000s, Doug Cutting and Mike Cafarella invented the Hadoop Distributed File System (HDFS) at Yahoo!. Hadoop (*https://oreil.ly/NFzbt*) provided a highly distributed and user-configurable way to store data at scale. One of the unique aspects of Hadoop was that it did not try to couple the query engine (how data was retrieved from it) with how the data was stored. Let's unpack that idea a little bit to clearly understand some of the differences between Hadoop and its predecessors.

In a traditional relational database management system (RDBMS), the database engine provides a set of abstractions to order the data. These abstractions are known as databases, schemas, and tables. Users can use these abstractions to store, augment, and retrieve data. Additionally, the database query engine is optimized to retrieve data based on abstractions. Databases like MySQL and Postgres use these abstractions, and if you've worked on a web application, you've likely used one of these databases as a backend.

A key component to the design of the original RDBMS was data locality. Data stored in these systems resided on the same machine where the query engine was and where queries were executed. The advantage of this architecture is that it requires minimal orchestration to retrieve data. When a user queries data in an RDBMS, all the data is stored on the machine disk and retrieved. Contrast this with HDFS. When a user asks for data, data may be stored across several machines, and orchestration is required to retrieve the data.

One convenient aspect of the RDBMS, and perhaps its lasting legacy, is Structured Query Language (SQL). SQL provides a convenient dialect for describing, manipulating, and retrieving data. In the early days of Hadoop, an interface like SQL did not exist for retrieving data from HDFS. Instead, users wrote MapReduce jobs that provided a low-level abstraction to retrieving and manipulating data. After several years of MapReduce, Hive, a SQL interface for Hadoop, was born. Hive improved the usability of HDFS considerably. Now, anyone with knowledge of SQL could retrieve data from HDFS, and the necessity for specialized developers who knew MapReduce was minimized. The way Hive worked is that it utilized metadata about the data stored in HDFS to create catalogs, and then those catalogs could be queried by SQL with the right parsers (see Figure 10-3).

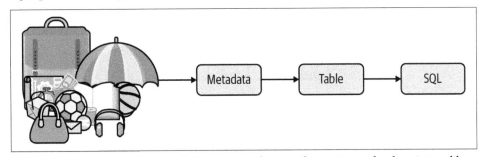

Figure 10-3. Given raw data, utilizing its metadata, and organizing the data into tables, we can use SQL to query it. SQL-on-Anything engines use this technique to query data ranging from event streams to CSV files.

Since the release of Hive, several open source projects were born to address some of its problems that were never overcome by the Hive SQL query engine itself: namely, poor performance and a complex deployment topology. Presto and Spark are two of the most notable projects that fit this classification. Presto and Spark were initially designed to solve the problems found with Hive (or querying distributed data more broadly). However, as the industry moves to new tools like object storage and streaming platforms, the need to provide a SQL engine over data stored in these systems was apparent. Spark and Presto are known as SQL-on-Anything engines today. They provide SQL over several other systems. For Pulsar, Presto provides a SQL engine over Pulsar topics, and that effort is known as Pulsar SQL.

Apache Flink: An Alternative Perspective

Apache Flink is an open source stream and batch processing engine. Flink is not a SQL-on-Anything engine. Still, I believe that spending a little bit of time talking about Flink's differences should crystallize the value of the SQL-on-Anything engine.

Flink's specialty is querying messaging systems or events. While Flink can be used as a general-purpose engine to query flat files like Hive or Spark, this isn't where it shines. In addition, Flink utilizes type systems and serialization to expose arbitrary message data as a table. Flink SQL is a SQL engine for Flink that builds on the streams as tables concept to offer a simple SQL language for querying event data (see Figure 10-4).

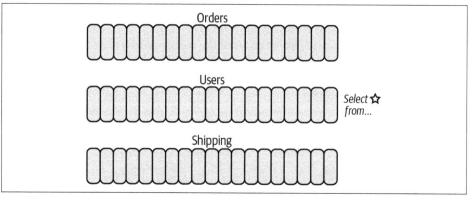

Figure 10-4. In Apache Flink, SQL users can query any stream with an ANSI SQL syntax, bringing table semantics to unbounded streams.

Flink SQL looks just like SQL over streams of data:

```
SELECT select_list FROM table_expression [ WHERE boolean_expression ]
```

If we analyze Flink SQL, we can see that instead of being a SQL-on-Anything engine, it's deliberately a SQL-on-Streams engine. For Pulsar, Flink SQL is an appropriate alternative to the Presto implementation of Pulsar SQL. Why does Pulsar use Presto instead of Flink for SQL implementation? The main reason is that Presto is embeddable. This means you can run Presto alongside a Pulsar deployment. To contrast this with Flink SQL, a deployment would require an eternal deployment of Flink to enable Flink SQL.

Presto/Trino

Presto is a distributed SQL-on-Everything engine developed at Facebook. Presto's initial scope was as a distributed query engine for Hadoop; however, due to its pluggable architecture and few moving parts, it has evolved to be the query engine for any system (with a bit of work).

Trino is a fork of Presto. Without getting too involved, Presto is open source but managed by Facebook. Since Presto was made freely available, many companies have gotten involved with the project, suggesting improvements and contributing code. Ultimately, Facebook decides what goes into Presto and what doesn't, and some Presto contributors grew tired of Presto's ownership and forked the project. The project is now Trino, and Trino is housed in an open source foundation called the PrestoDB Foundation.

Every project that utilized Presto had to decide whether it would stay with the Facebook version of Presto or move to Trino. Apache Pulsar decided to go with Trino, and so throughout the rest of the book, I'll refer to Presto as "Trino."

How Pulsar SQL Works

At its heart, Pulsar SQL is an implementation of a Trino connector. The Trino connector acts as a Pulsar consumer, utilizing metadata stored about each topic to effectively query data (see Figure 10-5).

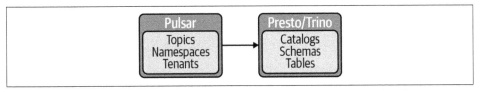

Figure 10-5. A high-level view of Pulsar SQL. Pulsar concepts are translated to Trino concepts and executed by Trino.

Trino, like Pulsar, is a distributed system with many components. Trino clusters have a few responsibilities, including the following:

- Querying data from external sources
- Coordinating distributed work
- Managing user permissions
- Caching data
- Storing metadata

A Trino cluster has worker nodes that interact with external systems, coordinators that manage orchestration for work, and meta stores to manage the internal representation of data. Figure 10-6 provides a representation of a Trino cluster.

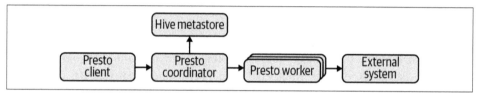

Figure 10-6. In a Trino cluster, worker nodes interact with external systems, coordinators manage orchestration for work, and meta stores manage the internal representation of data.

When implementing a Pulsar SQL interface, we have two options. One option is to read data from the topic, like a Pulsar client would (see Figure 10-7). The other is to read directly from where the data is stored in Pulsar (BookKeeper for most data and object storage for any offloaded data). Let's talk about the trade-offs of each approach.

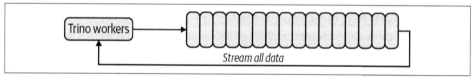

Figure 10-7. In this example, the entire topic is streamed out to Trino for processing on every request.

As we've discussed, Pulsar is novel in that it separates storage from other needs in the system through BookKeeper. In addition to being separate, BookKeeper storage is also redundant, in that the same ledger is stored across multiple bookies. Storing the data across multiple bookies makes it possible to parallelize queries to retrieve the data as well (see Figure 10-8).

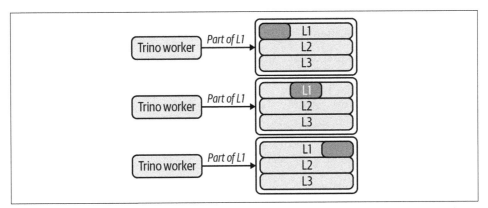

Figure 10-8. A group of Trino workers retrieving data from Ledger 1 (L1). Each worker can retrieve only parts of the ledger, and then bring the parts back together, decreasing retrieval time.

We've also talked about how Pulsar SQL retrieves data from object storage (for tiered storage) and how Trino (*https://oreil.ly/WmTep*) already supports a highly parallelized and performant implementation for reading from S3. All told, Trino is the perfect engine for retrieving data from Pulsar, since retrieving data is not a stream processing job, but more of an information retrieval job (see Figure 10-9).

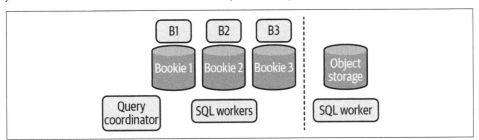

Figure 10-9. Trino utilizes the Pulsar architecture to provide performant information retrieval that can be easily parallelized.

Configuring Pulsar SQL

By default, Pulsar ships with an embedded Trino instance. Including Trino as a default option enables users who are new to Pulsar SQL to use Trino without standing up a Trino cluster. In this section, we'll focus on the embedded version of Pulsar SQL. If you're interested in deploying your own Trino cluster to run Pulsar SQL, I recommend following the instructions in the Pulsar documentation (*https://oreil.ly/W2uzb*).

To configure Pulsar SQL, we need to edit the *pulsar.properties* file, which can be found at the following location:

```
${project.root}/conf/presto/catalog/pulsar.properties
```

The *pulsar.properties* file looks like this:

```
# name of the connector to be displayed in the catalog
connector.name=pulsar

# the url of Pulsar broker service
pulsar.web-service-url=http://localhost:8080

# URI of Zookeeper cluster
pulsar.zookeeper-uri=localhost:2181

# minimum number of entries to read at a single time
pulsar.entry-read-batch-size=100

# default number of splits to use per query
pulsar.target-num-splits=4
```

If you have multiple Pulsar brokers, you can configure them in the following way:

```
pulsar.web-service-url=http://localhost:8080,localhost:8081,localhost:8082
pulsar.zookeeper-uri=localhost1,localhost2:2181
```

To start a Pulsar SQL cluster, you can use the CLI tools:

```
$ ./bin/pulsar sql-worker -help
Usage: launcher [options] command

Commands: run, start, stop, restart, kill, status

Options:
  -h, --help              show this help message and exit
  -v, --verbose           Run verbosely
  --etc-dir=DIR           Defaults to INSTALL_PATH/etc
  --launcher-config=FILE
                          Defaults to INSTALL_PATH/bin/launcher.properties
  --node-config=FILE      Defaults to ETC_DIR/node.properties
  --jvm-config=FILE       Defaults to ETC_DIR/jvm.config
  --config=FILE           Defaults to ETC_DIR/config.properties
  --log-levels-file=FILE
                          Defaults to ETC_DIR/log.properties
  --data-dir=DIR          Defaults to INSTALL_PATH
  --pid-file=FILE         Defaults to DATA_DIR/var/run/launcher.pid
  --launcher-log-file=FILE
                          Defaults to DATA_DIR/var/log/launcher.log (only in
                          daemon mode)
  --server-log-file=FILE
                          Defaults to DATA_DIR/var/log/server.log (only in
                          daemon mode)
  -D NAME=VALUE           Set a Java system property
```

To start Pulsar SQL, you can run the following command:

```
$ ./bin/pulsar sql-worker start
```

Let's run an end-to-end example to show how Pulsar SQL works.

Publish data to a topic:

```
public class Test {

    public static class Person {
        private int id = 1;
        private String name;
        private long date;
    }

    public static void main(String[] args) throws Exception {
        PulsarClient pulsarClient = PulsarClient.builder()
          .serviceUrl("pulsar://localhost:6650").build();
        Producer<Person> producer = pulsarClient
          .newProducer(AvroSchema.of(Person.class)).topic("person_topic")
          .create();

        for (int i = 0; i < 1000; i++) {
            Person person = new Person();
            person.setid(i);
            person.setname("foo" + i);
            person.setdate(System.currentTimeMillis());
            producer.newMessage().value(person).send();
        }
        producer.close();
        pulsarClient.close();
    }
}
```

Start Pulsar SQL:

```
./bin/pulsar sql-worker run
```

Start the Pulsar cluster:

```
./bin/pulsar sql
```

Check that our data is in the catalog:

```
show tables in pulsar."public/default";
```

This returns person_topic.

Query our data:

```
select * from pulsar."public/default".person_topic;
```

This returns 1,000 rows of our generated data. Since we are no longer adding data to the topic, we see a static view. If we were to continually stream new data in our query, it would result in an infinite stream of records.

To recap, as long as we provide a type (Pojo, Avro, JSON, etc.) to our data, Pulsar SQL can expose our streams as tables. This is a powerful idea and useful for powering a number of applications, including dashboards and real-time systems.

Performance Considerations

We talked a little about how Trino works, and it's worth learning what the performance of Pulsar SQL will look like at scale.

The parallel architecture of Trino and the parallelism offered by BookKeeper and cloud object storage means that Trino is reliably scalable both horizontally and vertically. As we add more bookies and more object storage (for tiered storage), we can continue to scale our Trino cluster and keep performance for Pulsar SQL queries in lockstep with our needs.

In some real-world scenarios, Pulsar SQL has been measurably fast. Table 10-1 summarizes these performance metrics.[2]

Table 10-1. Pulsar SQL performance metrics

Configuration	JSON (compressed) parsing performance	Avro (compressed) parsing performance
3 nodes 12 CPU cores 128 GB RAM 2X1.2 TB NVME disks	~ 60 million rows per second	~ 50 million rows per second

Summary

This chapter covered the use cases for Pulsar SQL, and detailed the Pulsar SQL architecture and the steps for setting up Pulsar SQL in a Pulsar cluster to emphasize the value of having an interchangeable method between streams and tables. Pulsar SQL is the final mechanism for communicating with Pulsar that we'll cover in this book. For the remaining three chapters, we'll talk about the following:

- Deploying Pulsar in various environments
- Operating Pulsar
- My thoughts on the future of Pulsar

---

2 From the talk "Interactive querying of streams using Apache Pulsar" by Jerry Peng (*https://oreil.ly/CkYlE*).

## CHAPTER 11

Deploying Pulsar

A discussion of Pulsar would be incomplete without talking about Pulsar deployment. Deploying Pulsar exposes the operator to many of the lower-level constructs in Pulsar and helps them find some of the patterns in the process. This chapter will cover several ways to deploy Pulsar, including Docker, Kubernetes, and bare metal.

Docker

The simplest way to get up and running with Pulsar is by utilizing the official Pulsar Docker image(s). The Docker deployment is still necessary to deploy all the Pulsar components, including Apache ZooKeeper and Apache BookKeeper, but the official Pulsar images from Docker Hub ease the burden (see Figure 11-1).

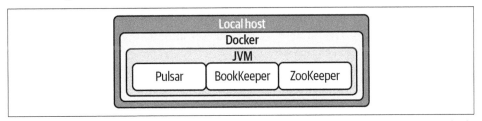

Figure 11-1. Pulsar running on Docker. The host system runs the Docker daemon, which runs a virtualized environment with the Java virtual machine. The Pulsar nodes, Apache BookKeeper, and Apache ZooKeeper run within the virtualized environment.

Docker is an excellent way to get started because it doesn't require you to install anything in your local environment (other than Docker, of course). It also works across multiple systems, including macOS, Windows, and various flavors of Linux. When getting started with any system, I generally recommend starting with Docker before moving to anything else.

To get started with the Docker deployment, we first need to pull all images related to Pulsar from Docker Hub:

```
docker pull apachepulsar/pulsar-all:latest
```

This command pulls images for Pulsar, ZooKeeper, and BookKeeper. From here, we should run each image.

```
docker run -it --name bookkeeper apachepulsar/pulsar-all:latest /bin/bash docker
run -it --name zookeeper apachepulsar/pulsar-all:latest /bin/bash docker run -it --
name broker apachepulsar/pulsar-all:latest /bin/bash
```

Next, we need to create network connectivity between the Docker images. We'll create a Pulsar network and then connect each container to the network.

First, create the network:

```
docker network create Pulsar
```

Then connect each image to the network:

```
docker network connect pulsar zookeeper
docker network connect pulsar bookkeeper
docker network connect pulsar broker
```

With that command, we've built a Pulsar cluster from Docker containers. We can add another container to the Pulsar network or port forward traffic from the containers to the localhost to connect to the cluster.

One alternative to this path is to use Docker Compose. Docker Compose provides a mechanism to deploy multiple components in Docker and orchestrate their deployment. The Pulsar open source project has a helpful Docker Compose implementation.

Docker Compose deploys the following (you can remove elements that are not necessary for your use case). The numbers in parentheses indicate the number of containers that are deployed for each service:

- ZooKeeper (3)
- BookKeeper (3)
- Pulsar (3)
- Proxy (1)
- WebSocket (1)
- Function (1)
- Pulsar Manager (1)
- SQL (1)

To get started we need to clone the Pulsar repository:

```
git clone https://github.com/apache/pulsar.git
```

Next, we need to get to the directory with the Docker Compose configuration:

```
cd docker-compose/kitchen-sink
```

Now we just run the compose file:

```
docker-compose up
```

Once all the resources are deployed, we can begin sending messages to Pulsar as well as interacting with the admin console.

Bare Metal

In this section, when I use the term *bare metal* I mean deploying in an environment that is outside the public cloud. There is some debate about whether bare metal means a nonvirtualized environment, but we'll stick to the nonpublic cloud definition for this section.

To deploy Pulsar on bare metal, we need to deploy each of the following in the order presented:

- Apache ZooKeeper cluster
- Initialized cluster metadata
- Apache BookKeeper cluster
- A minimum of one Pulsar broker

In earlier chapters, we talked about how both Pulsar brokers and BookKeeper bookies use Apache ZooKeeper. In some deployments, you may want to deploy two ZooKeeper clusters for dedicated responsibility, but we'll share ZooKeeper across Pulsar nodes and bookies for our use case.

Minimum Requirements

For the bare-bones Pulsar deployment, only six virtual machines are needed. Ideally, these virtual machines are Linux based and have the 64-bit JRE/JDK 8 or later installed.

Hardware requirements may vary, but it's recommended to have at least 1 TB of disk space per virtual machine, 16 virtual CPUs, and about 100 GB of RAM for production workloads.

Getting Started

Once your virtual machines are provisioned, you should install the most recent Pulsar binaries (Pulsar 2.8.0 at the time of this writing). You can install the binaries using wget:

```
wget https://archive.apache.org/dist/pulsar/pulsar-2.8.0/apache-pulsar-2.8.0-bin.tar.gz
```

Once you've downloaded wget, untar the binary in preparation for the installation:

```
$ tar xvzf apache-pulsar-2.8.0-bin.tar.gz $ cd apache-pulsar-2.8.0
```

Table 11-1 summarizes the directories in the Pulsar distribution.

Table 11-1. Common directories in the Pulsar distribution

Directory	Purpose
bin	This directory contains all the command-line tools, such as Pulsar and pulsar-admin. You'll use these tools as we install Pulsar and its various components.
conf	This directory contains all the configuration files for Pulsar, ZooKeeper, and BookKeeper.
data	This directory is the data storage directory for Apache ZooKeeper and BookKeeper.
lib	This directory contains all the JAR files used in Pulsar.
logs	This directory contains all the logs created when interacting with installation files.

Deploying ZooKeeper

On three of our virtual machines, we'll perform the following steps. Since ZooKeeper is responsible for most of the coordination tasks in Pulsar and BookKeeper, we need to make sure ZooKeeper is installed and running before moving forward.

To begin, we need to ensure that each node has the same ZooKeeper configuration:

```
cd conf
vi zookeeper.conf

server.1=zk1.us-west.example.com:2888:3888
server.2=zk2.us-west.example.com:2888:3888
server.3=zk3.us-west.example.com:2888:3888
```

Additionally, each ZooKeeper node must have an ID parameter set. We create this ID in the *data/zookeeper* directory on each node as follows:

```
mkdir -p data/zookeeper
echo <id> > data/zookeeper/myid
```

Now we're ready to start ZooKeeper. Since we're going to install bookies on these same nodes, we need to change the ZooKeeper stats port in our command to start ZooKeeper:

```
PULSAR_EXTRA_OPTS="-Dstats_server_port=8001" bin/pulsar-daemon start zookeeper
```

We also need to initialize our Pulsar cluster:

```
$ bin/pulsar initialize-cluster-metadata \
--cluster pulsar-cluster-1 \
--zookeeper zk1.us-west.example.com:2181 \
--configuration-store zk1.us-west.example.com:2181 \
--web-service-url http://pulsar.us-west.example.com:8080 \
--web-service-url-tls https://pulsar.us-west.example.com:8443 \
--broker-service-url pulsar://pulsar.us-west.example.com:6650 \
--broker-service-url-tls pulsar+ssl://pulsar.us-west.example.com:6651
```

This command tells ZooKeeper where to find specific pieces of metadata about the Pulsar cluster. For it to work, the operator needs to have a DNS server and configure traffic to route to these URLs, TLS termination, and other considerations.

Starting BookKeeper

Now that ZooKeeper is operating and the cluster metadata is initialized, we need to get our bookies up and running. On the same nodes that we installed ZooKeeper, let's install bookies.

The first step is to configure the bookies, similar to what we did with ZooKeeper. *conf/bookkeeper* confuses the host/port configurations we used in the ZooKeeper configuration section. It should look like this:

```
zkServers=zk1.us-west.example.com:2181,
zk2.us-west.example.com:2181,
zk3.us-west.example.com:2181
```

BookKeeper has many configurable values, but for this installation, all of the defaults are satisfactory. Next, we use the pulsar-daemon command-line tool to start the bookies one at a time:

```
$ bin/pulsar-daemon start bookie
```

We can validate the installation by using the *bookiesanity* tool:

```
$ bin/bookkeeper shell bookiesanity
```

If successful, we validated our install of BookKeeper.

Starting Pulsar

Similar to BookKeeper and ZooKeeper, all of Pulsar's configurations are in the */conf* directory; specifically, the */conf/broker.conf* files. First, we need to make sure our Zoo-Keeper servers and configuration servers match what we included in the previous sections:

```
zookeeperServers=zk1.us-west.example.com:2181,
zk2.us-west.example.com:2181,
zk3.us-west.example.com:2181
  configurationStoreServers=zk1.us-west.example.com:2181,
```

```
zk2.us-west.example.com:2181,
zk3.us-west.example.com:2181
```

Our cluster name should also match what we set when we initialized the cluster metadata:

```
clusterName=pulsar-cluster-1
```

Additionally, we need to verify that our values for ports match what was set in the cluster initialization:

```
brokerServicePort=6650
brokerServicePortTls=6651
webServicePort=8080
webServicePortTls=8443
```

Now we're ready to start our Pulsar cluster; we can do this by using the pulsar-daemon command-line tool:

```
bin/pulsar-daemon start broker
```

Now that we have a running Pulsar cluster, we should confirm that it works according to our specifications. You can use a Pulsar client and connect to the broker service URL, or you can use the command-line tool that ships with Pulsar. You first need to change the Pulsar client configuration located in *conf/client* from whichever Pulsar node you decide to run in *conf/client.conf*:

```
webServiceUrl=http://us-west.example.com:8080
   brokerServiceurl=pulsar://us-west.example.com:6650
```

Now we can send some data to Pulsar:

```
$ bin/pulsar-client produce \
  persistent://public/default/test \
  -n 1 \
  -m "Hello, moto"
```

We can open a new client to consume the message:

```
$ bin/pulsar-client consume \
  persistent://public/default/test \
  -n 100 \
  -s "consumer-test" \
```

Installing Pulsar on bare metal is a considerable amount of work, and without proper configuration tools, it is also prone to mistakes and frustration. It's recommended that you use a tool like Ansible to automate much of the work described in this section. I'll go into what that looks like in the next section on public cloud installations.

Public Cloud Providers

Nowadays, a likely mechanism for deploying Pulsar is the public cloud. There are many good reasons to deploy Pulsar on the public cloud; one of the biggest is using the cloud platform. An additional reason that is especially relevant for us is the elasticity of the cloud. Getting started with a small implementation and deployment and then expanding later is entirely possible.

This section will cover some of the high-level differences between the three major cloud providers when deploying Apache Pulsar. Before we dive into the specifics of each cloud provider, I need to introduce some tools that have not been discussed in the book so far.

We'll use two tools to deploy Pulsar into the public cloud providers: Terraform and Ansible.

Terraform is an "infrastructure as code" tool. It provides some building blocks to connect to public resources (like cloud providers and software as a service vendors) and provision them. At its core, Terraform is relatively simple. It provides a handful of valuable abstractions over your infrastructure. First, it keeps track of the current state of your infrastructure (see Figure 11-2). Second, it provides a schema over infrastructure objects, and finally, it provides an authentication mechanism to apply those changes.

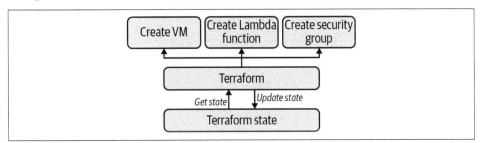

Figure 11-2. Terraform provides "infrastructure as code" tools to deploy and control cloud software. Users can track the state of their applications in the cloud, inventory them, and delete them.

Ansible is a tool for managing configurations, deploying applications, and checking the current state of the process (see Figure 11-3). Whereas Terraform is about working with third-party systems like AWS to request resources, Ansible configures those resources after they are provisioned.

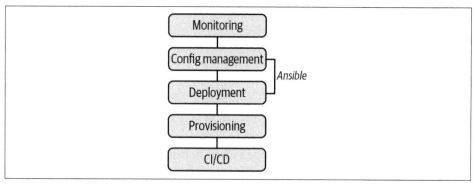

Figure 11-3. Ansible sits in the configuration management and deployment plane of DevOps. You can use Ansible to automate tasks like setting up servers and deploying binaries.

We'll use Terraform to provide the resources needed for each cloud provider and then Ansible to install and configure Pulsar.

AWS

Pulsar ships with Terraform and Ansible modules; to use them, you need to have the following installed on your system:

- AWS command-line tool (you must be authenticated)
- Python 3.7
- PIP (Python package manager)
- Terraform
- Ansible

To get started, clone the Pulsar GitHub repository with the Terraform and Ansible code:

```
git clone https://github.com/apache/pulsar
cd pulsar/deployment/terraform-ansible/aws
```

Next, initialize Terraform from this repository:

```
terraform init
```

Apply the default configurations included in the repository:

```
terraform apply
```

If you inspect your Terraform response, you should see the following resources deployed in the us-west-2 region of AWS:

- 9 EC2 instances
  - Three t2.small instances
  - Three i3.xlarge instances
  - Two c5.2xlarge instances
  - One c5.2xlarge instance
- A security group
- A virtual private cloud
- An API gateway
- A route table
- A subnet for the virtual private cloud (VPC)

Now we can use Ansible to install Pulsar, BookKeeper, and ZooKeeper.

First we'll use the Ansible Playbook to configure the disks for BookKeeper:

```
ansible-playbook \
  --user='ec2-user' \
  --inventory=`which terraform-inventory` \
  setup-disk.yaml
```

Next we'll use the Ansible Playbook to set up Pulsar. This will perform all the steps in the bare metal installation. It may take a few minutes for everything to become operational:

```
ansible-playbook \ --user='ec2-user' \ --inventory=`which terraform-inventory` \
../deploy-pulsar.yaml
```

We can validate our Pulsar installation by trying to connect to the Pulsar cluster and sending some messages:

```
$ pip install pulsar-client

$ python
import pulsar
client = pulsar.Client('pulsar://pulsar-client-url')
producer = client.create_producer('persistent://public/default/test-topic')
producer.send('Hello, moto')
>>> client.close()
```

Azure

Installing Pulsar on Azure is very similar to installing it on AWS. This section will point out only places where the process is meaningfully different from the AWS process.

The requirements to install from your local system are as follows:

- Azure CLI (you must be authenticated)
- Python 3.7
- PIP (Python package manager)
- Terraform
- Ansible

You will need to perform the same Terraform commands you performed for AWS; the only difference is you need to clone it from a different place. By default, Azure Terraform is not included in the Pulsar repository:

```
git clone https://github.com/josep2/pulsar-ias
cd pulsar/deployment/terraform-ansible/azure
```

From here, you can follow the steps in the AWS installation.

Google Cloud Platform

Installing Pulsar on Google Cloud is very similar to installing it on AWS. This section will point out only places where the process is meaningfully different from the AWS process.

The requirements to install from your local system are as follows:

- Google Cloud CLI (you must be authenticated)
- Python 3.7
- PIP (Python package manager)
- Terraform
- Ansible

You will need to perform the same Terraform commands as you did in the AWS section; the only difference is you need to clone it from a different place. By default, GCP Terraform is not included in the Pulsar repository:

```
git clone https://github.com/josep2/pulsar-ias
cd pulsar/deployment/terraform-ansible/gcp
```

From here, you can follow the steps in the AWS installation.

Kubernetes

Since its public release in 2014, Kubernetes has become an increasingly popular mechanism for operating software in production environments. Kubernetes provides a set of abstractions that hide much of the complexity of deploying containerized applications. The popularity and rise of Kubernetes are also partially because of its ease of running in a local environment. For many Kubernetes applications, you can use minikube. A local virtualized clustered environment, minikube is an excellent way to get a feel for how a workload would run on Kubernetes before releasing it into your production environment.

Deploying an application in a Kubernetes cluster requires the operator to tell the Kubernetes API what they wish to deploy. "What" can include anything from which container Kubernetes should deploy to managing events like rollbacks and data backups. Kubernetes is flexible, but it requires users to describe their deployments with YAML or JSON. Kubernetes provides default APIs to use and lets the end user customize and provide their objects and operator patterns. With all of this choice and sprawling API definitions, Kubernetes deployments can quickly become unwieldy. Helm is a project designed to deal with some of the problems created by Kubernetes deployment. Helm is described as a "package manager for Kubernetes." It provides some abstractions (on top of the dense existing Kubernetes abstractions) to simplify Kubernetes deployments.

For Apache Pulsar deployments on Kubernetes, Helm is the recommended way to accomplish this. Kubernetes is a popular way to deploy Pulsar because Pulsar has a project that has actively looked to Kubernetes to serve as the infrastructure layer for many components. In Chapter 8 we talked about Pulsar Functions on Kubernetes, and there are many efforts to make BookKeeper and ZooKeeper run better on Kubernetes.

This section will walk through all the requirements to deploy an Apache Pulsar Helm chart. Helm uses templates to capture all the configurations across a deployment. The Helm chart has many default values, so we typically don't have to set anything to get started. However, you can look to this version of the entire helm chart with notes from the maintainers on each of the values for reference.

Before using Helm, you should have kubectl and helm installed in your local environment. For local Kubernetes, some projects that are helpful are:

- minikube (*https://oreil.ly/kfIoo*)
- Kind (*https://oreil.ly/wSGXs*)
- Docker for Desktop (*https://oreil.ly/kYH0c*)

To prepare for a Helm release, you can run the following command:

```
git clone https://github.com/apache/pulsar-helm-chart cd pulsar-helm-chart
./scripts/pulsar/prepare_helm_release.sh -n <k8s-namespace> -k <helm-release-name>
```

This will create all of the following resources:

- A Kubernetes namespace for installing the Pulsar release.
- JSON Web Tokens (JWT) secret keys and tokens for three super users: broker-admin, proxy-admin, and admin. By default, it generates an asymmetric public/private key pair. You can choose to generate a symmetric secret key by specifying `--symmetric`.

    — The proxy-admin role is used for proxies to communicate to brokers.

    — The broker-admin role is used for inter-broker communications.

    — The admin tools use the admin role.

Now we can install the chart:

```
helm repo add apache https://pulsar.apache.org/charts helm repo update helm install
pulsar apache/pulsar \ --timeout 10m \ --set initialize=true \ --set [any other
configuration values]
```

After deployment, it may take up to 10 minutes for all the components to be available. You can always check the status of your deployment with:

```
helm status pulsar
```

Some common errors you'll see are pods that are in a `ContainerCreating` state or a `CrashloopBackoff` state. This typically means that not all of the components are executed in order and they will restart until things are working properly. Other times there may be issues in your Kubernetes cluster setup, and it may help to delete your Helm installation and try again.

While the Kubernetes mechanism for deployment required learning a few abstractions, all of the work required on our end involved changing configuration values. I believe this is a fair trade-off, and for an organization that is already using Kubernetes, deploying Pulsar on Kubernetes is an effective way to get started.

Summary

In this chapter we covered several mechanisms for deploying Apache Pulsar. How you choose to deploy Pulsar will depend on your organizational expertise as well as your patience. Now we have sufficient context to take the next (and final) step in our journey, that of operating our cluster. In Chapter 12 you'll learn about:

- Metrics collection in Pulsar
- Performance tuning
- Interceptors
- Metrics forwarding

Operating Pulsar

As you saw in Chapter 11, deploying Pulsar can take some effort, but how can we ensure its reliability once it's deployed and in use? First, we need to be able to measure aspects of our system. Second, we need to understand the metrics in isolation. Third, we need to understand the interaction between metrics. And finally, we need to be able to understand when the preceding points deviate from our expectations. If we take a step back to consider everything required to operate a system successfully, it may be overwhelming to us. Fortunately, Pulsar makes metrics collection simple by providing a slew of metrics by default. This chapter will walk through those metrics and provide some context on which metrics are helpful to keep an eye on if you're new to operating Apache Pulsar.

Before we explore each section, it's essential to understand the types of metrics provided by Pulsar:

Counter
> A counter is a cumulative metric, and it increases monotonically. Counters help visualize the total number of a metric occurring over a given duration.

Gauge
> A gauge represents a single numeric value. Gauges are suitable for representing what is going on at the exact moment versus a historical look.

Histogram
> A histogram is a sampled representation of observations. A histogram is suitable for getting counts of metrics in a specific bucket of time.

Summary
> A summary is a histogram over a sliding window.

Apache BookKeeper Metrics

Apache BookKeeper is the storage engine for Pulsar, and as it is a critical component, understanding its behavior is paramount. BookKeeper metrics break down into three categories:

Server metrics
Metrics concerning the bookie (BookKeeper server)

Journal metrics
Metrics concerning the read/write operations of the bookie's journal

Storage metrics
Metrics concerning how much data is stored on the bookie

We'll walk through all of these metrics and discuss which are the most valuable to get started in monitoring Pulsar.

Server Metrics

Server metrics provide some key metrics around the BookKeeper server status. They can tell you things like the following:

- Whether the bookie is available in read or write mode
- How many ADD_ENTRY requests are going to the bookie
- The number of READ BYTES the bookie is processing

These metrics are helpful in managing the day-to-day operations of BookKeeper as well as diagnosing problems in the event of an outage. Following is a list of server metrics:

bookie_SERVER_STATUS *(Gauge)*
This metric can have one of two values:

- 1 means the bookie is running in a writable mode.
- 0 means the bookie is running in a read-only mode.

Many of the bookie metrics are about the size of data transfer. This metric is valuable to ensure that all bookies are in a writable mode before troubleshooting any further.

bookkeeper_server_ADD_ENTRY_count *(Counter)*
This metric represents the total number of ADD_ENTRY requests received by the bookie.

`bookkeeper_server_READ_ENTRY_count` *(Counter)*
: This metric represents the total number of READ_ENTRY requests received by the bookie.

`bookie_WRITE_BYTES` *(Counter)*
: This metric represents the cumulative bytes written to a bookie.

`bookie_READ_BYTES` *(Counter)*
: This metric represents the cumulative bytes read from a bookie.

`bookkeeper_server_ADD_ENTRY_REQUEST` *(Summary)*
: This metric represents the request latency for ADD_ENTRY requests for a bookie. It will tell you approximately how long it takes to fulfill an ADD_ENTRY request. This is a good metric to keep a close eye on because increased latency here is a good indication of an underprovisioned bookie.

`bookkeeper_server_READ_ENTRY_REQUEST` *(Summary)*
: This metric represents the request latency for READ_ENTRY requests for a bookie. It will tell you approximately how long it takes to fulfill a READ_ENTRY request. We expect this metric to be consistent but highly correlated with consumer activity in the cluster.

Journal Metrics

Journal metrics provide some detailed metrics on a per-bookie basis. They tell you things like:

- Journal queue size
- Journal latency when syncing
- Journal request latency

These metrics can be critical when diagnosing problems around end-to-end performance with BookKeeper. Journal metrics include the following:

`bookie_journal_JOURNAL_SYNC_count` *(Counter)*
: This metric represents the total number of journal *fsync* operations occurring on the bookie.

`bookie_journal_JOURNAL_QUEUE_SIZE` *(Gauge)*
: This metric represents the number of pending requests waiting to be appended to the bookie journal. This is a good metric to watch closely because when this queue gets large, it's an indication that there may be problems somewhere within the system.

bookie_journal_JOURNAL_FORCE_WRITE_QUEUE_SIZE *(Gauge)*
This metric represents the total number of *fsync* requests pending in the write queue.

bookie_journal_JOURNAL_CB_QUEUE_SIZE *(Gauge)*
This metric represents the total number of callbacks pending in the callback queue.

bookie_journal_JOURNAL_ADD_ENTRY *(Summary)*
This metric provides the request latency of appending new entries to the journal.

bookie_journal_JOURNAL_SYNC *(Summary)*
This metric summarizes the *fsync* latency of syncing data to the journal's disk.

Storage Metrics

Storage metrics tell you statistics about how much a bookie is storing on a few dimensions. Storage metrics can provide insight into the following:

- Total number of ledgers
- Total number of entries
- Write and read cache

These metrics are valuable for diagnosing that everything is working properly as well as knowing when to add additional bookies to the cluster. They include the following:

bookie_ledgers_count *(Gauge)*
This metric counts the total number of ledgers stored in the bookie.

bookie_entries_count *(Gauge)*
This metric counts the total number of entries stored within a bookie.

bookie_write_cache_size *(Gauge)*
This metric is a count of the total bookie write cache size in bytes.

bookie_read_cache_size *(Gauge)*
This metric is a count of the total bookie read cache size in bytes.

bookie_DELETED_LEDGER_COUNT *(Counter)*
This metric represents the total number of ledgers that the bookie has deleted.

bookie_ledger_writable_dirs *(Gauge)*
This metric represents the total number of writable directories available on the bookie.

Apache ZooKeeper Metrics

Apache ZooKeeper stores metadata for both BookKeeper and Pulsar; a Pulsar deployment would not work correctly without a fully operational ZooKeeper cluster. There are two types of ZooKeeper metrics:

Server metrics
   Metrics about specific behavior related to the ZooKeeper deployment topology

Request metrics
   Metrics concerning the rate and volume of data arriving at and leaving the ZooKeeper cluster

This section explains these metrics and how to use them to monitor Pulsar effectively. We'll cover metrics forwarding later in this chapter; for now, note that ZooKeeper metrics can all be forwarded to Prometheus (see Figure 12-1).

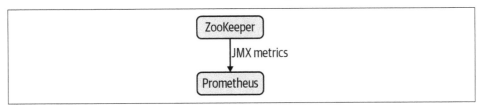

Figure 12-1. Java Management Extensions (JMX) metrics are collected by Prometheus, a time series database and metrics server.

Server Metrics

Server metrics are another tool in our arsenal for ensuring that our ZooKeeper cluster is operational. Server metrics can tell you things like:

- How many z-nodes are in the cluster
- Active client connections
- The data storage on the nodes

This information is critical for a quick glance as well as useful to check in the event of an outage or performance degradation event. The server metrics on ZooKeeper include the following:

`zookeeper_server_znode_count` *(Gauge)*
   This metric represents is the total number of z-nodes stored in ZooKeeper.

`zookeeper_server_data_size_bytes` *(Gauge)*
   This metric is the total size (in bytes) of the z-nodes stored in ZooKeeper.

`zookeeper_server_connections` *(Gauge)*
> This metric represents the total number of open connections to ZooKeeper. It is helpful when debugging the connectivity of Pulsar nodes and bookies to Zoo-Keeper. This metric may be a leading indicator of bookies and Pulsar nodes going offline.

`zookeeper_server_watches_count` *(Gauge)*
> This metric represents the total number of watchers registered in ZooKeeper.

`zookeeper_server_ephemerals_count` *(Gauge)*
> This metric represents the total number of ephemeral z-nodes in ZooKeeper.

Request Metrics

Request metrics track the performance and load of ZooKeeper. Since ZooKeeper plays a critical role in tracking metadata around topics and how the data is stored, this is a critical metric to track. ZooKeeper request metrics include the following:

`zookeeper_server_requests` *(Counter)*
> This metric represents the total number of requests received by ZooKeeper.

`zookeeper_server_requests_latency_ms` *(Summary)*
> This metric summarizes the request latency (in milliseconds). It provides both the read and write latencies for ZooKeeper. Of all the metrics provided by Zoo-Keeper, this is perhaps the most valuable. Increased read and write latency outside of expectations with traffic is a good indication that something is wrong.

Topic Metrics

Topics are the units that Pulsar consumers and producers wish to monitor closely. For Pulsar topics, there are metrics around message egress and ingress, subscription counts, latencies, and size. Following is a list of each metric and some pointers that may be valuable when starting to monitor Pulsar:

`pulsar_subscriptions_count` *(Gauge)*
> This metric represents the number of subscriptions to the given topic. It is valuable for validating behavior in a Pulsar cluster. If subscription counts don't match what you expected from the number of consumers deployed, something may be amiss.

`pulsar_producers_count` *(Gauge)*
> This metric represents the number of active producers for a given topic.

`pulsar_consumers_count` *(Gauge)*
> This metric represents the number of active consumers for a topic.

`pulsar_rate_in` *(Gauge)*
> This metric represents the total message rate into Pulsar for the given topic, measured in messages per second.

`pulsar_rate_out` *(Gauge)*
> This metric represents the total message rate out of Pulsar for the given topic, measured in messages per second.

`pulsar_throughput_in` *(Gauge)*
> This metric represents the total throughput into Pulsar for the given topic, measured in bytes per second.

`pulsar_throughput_out` *(Gauge)*
> This metric represents the total throughput out of Pulsar for the given topic, measured in bytes per second.

`pulsar_storage_size` *(Gauge)*
> This metric represents the total size in bytes for the given Pulsar topic.

`pulsar_storage_backlog_size` *(Gauge)*
> This metric represents the total backlog size in messages for the given Pulsar topic.

`pulsar_storage_offloaded_size` *(Gauge)*
> This metric represents the total amount of data in bytes for the topic that has been offloaded to tiered storage.

`pulsar_storage_backlog_quota_limit` *(Gauge)*
> This metric represents the total amount of data (in bytes) that limits the backlog quota.

`pulsar_storage_write_rate` *(Gauge)*
> The metric represents the rate of message batches written to storage for the given topic, measured in message batches per second.

`pulsar_storage_read_rate` *(Gauge)*
> The metric represents the rate of message batches read from storage for the given topic, measured in message batches per second.

`pulsar_subscription_delayed` *(Gauge)*
> This metric represents the total number of message batches currently delayed from dispatching.

`pulsar_storage_write_latency_le_*` *(Histogram)*
> This metric represents the rate of messages above a specifically identified threshold.

`pulsar_entry_size_le_*` *(Histogram)*
This metric represents the rate of messages above a specifically identified size threshold (in bytes).

`pulsar_in_bytes_total` *(Counter)*
This metric represents the total number of bytes received for a topic.

`pulsar_in_messages_total` *(Counter)*
This metric represents the total number of messages received for a given topic.

`pulsar_out_bytes_total` *(Counter)*
This metric represents the total number of bytes read for a given topic.

`pulsar_out_messages_total` *(Counter)*
This metric represents the total number of messages read from a given topic.

Consumer Metrics

Misbehaving consumers are a concern for a Pulsar operator because a slow consumer can lead to a poor user experience and lost opportunity for streaming applications. Consumer metrics should ensure a smoothly operating Pulsar experience. Following is a list of consumer metrics for monitoring Pulsar:

`pulsar_consumer_msg_rate_redeliver` *(Gauge)*
This metric represents the total message rate per second being delivered to the consumer.

`pulsar_consumer_unacked_messages` *(Gauge)*
This metric represents the total number of unacknowledged messages for the consumer.

`pulsar_consumer_blocked_on_unacked_messages` *(Gauge)*
This metric represents whether a consumer is blocked because of unacknowledged messages. The metric can take one of two values:

- 1 means the consumer is blocked.
- 0 means the consumer is not blocked.

`pulsar_consumer_msg_throughput_out` *(Gauge)*
This metric represents the dispatch rate for the consumer, measured in messages per second.

`pulsar_consumer_msg_rate_out` *(Gauge)*
This metric represents the total dispatch throughout for a consumer, measured in bytes per second.

`pulsar_consumer_available_permits` *(Gauge)*
This metric represents the available permits for a consumer.

Pulsar Transaction Metrics

Transactions are a new feature introduced in Pulsar 2.8. Pulsar transactions provide some global consistency to consumers and are helpful for a vast number of real-time applications. That said, Pulsar transactions can fail or may be aborted by the producer, and any deviant behavior should be closely monitored. The following metrics are available for Pulsar transactions:

`pulsar_txn_active_count` *(Gauge)*
This metric represents the total number of active transactions for a given coordinator.

`pulsar_txn_created_count` *(Counter)*
This metric represents a count of the total number of transactions created.

`pulsar_txn_committed_count` *(Counter)*
This metric represents the total number of committed transactions.

`pulsar_txn_aborted_count` *(Counter)*
This metric represents the total number of transactions aborted for the given coordinator.

`pulsar_txn_timeout_count` *(Counter)*
This metric represents the total number of transactions that have timed out.

`pulsar_txn_append_log_count` *(Counter)*
This metric represents the total number of append transaction logs.

`pulsar_txn_execution_latency_le_*` *(Histogram)*
This metric represents the distribution of transaction time in milliseconds.

Pulsar Function Metrics

Pulsar Functions may be an integral part of your overall event processing system. As such, monitoring functions and ensuring that they behave according to our expectations is essential. Pulsar provides several metrics for Pulsar Functions that provide visibility into the functions' exceptions, throughput, and other custom metrics (see Figure 12-2). Following is a list of the Pulsar function metrics:

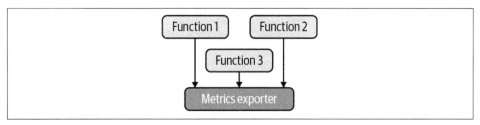

Figure 12-2. Each function exports its metrics independently and the metrics collector aggregates them.

`pulsar_function_processed_successfully_total` *(Counter)*
This metric represents the total number of messages processed successfully by the given Pulsar function.

`pulsar_function_processed_successfully_total_1min` *(Counter)*
This metric represents the total number of messages processed successfully over the last minute by a given Pulsar function.

`pulsar_function_system_exceptions_total` *(Counter)*
This metric represents the total number of exceptions in the system related to functions in the specified namespace.

`pulsar_function_system_exceptions_total_1min` *(Counter)*
This metric represents the total number of exceptions in the system related to functions in the specified namespace during the last 60-second interval.

`pulsar_function_user_exceptions_total` *(Counter)*
This metric represents the total number of user exceptions for functions in a given namespace.

`pulsar_function_user_exceptions_total_1min` *(Counter)*
This metric represents the total number of user exceptions for functions in a given namespace in the last 60-second interval.

`pulsar_function_process_latency_ms` *(Summary)*
This metric represents the latency of a process in milliseconds.

`pulsar_function_process_latency_ms_1min` *(Summary)*
This metric represents the latency of a process in milliseconds over the last 60-second interval.

`pulsar_function_last_invocation` *(Gauge)*
This metric represents the timestamp of the last invocation of the function.

`pulsar_function_received_total` *(Counter)*

This metric represents the total number of messages received from a source for a given function.

`pulsar_function_received_total_1min` *(Counter)*

This metric represents the total number of messages received from a source for a given function in the last 60-second interval.

`pulsar_function_user_metric_` *(Summary)*

This metric is reserved for user definition.

Advanced Operating Techniques

Operating Pulsar is equal parts good instrumentation (tracking the metrics just described) and experience (knowing what to look for). When attempting to provide trackable observability around a system, both breadth of metrics and an understanding of how they work in conjunction with one another is required. Pulsar provides a mechanism to get at that interaction point by enabling distributed tracing within a Pulsar system. Additionally, Pulsar provides a mechanism for exporting metrics to systems that are more suitable for analyzing the data extracted from Pulsar. We'll explore these features in detail in the following few subsections.

Interceptors and Tracing

One crucial consideration when monitoring an event streaming platform is understanding how messages traverse the system. In Pulsar, a message may start in a single topic and fan out over many more topics over time (see Figure 12-3). Obtaining a good grasp of the performance characteristics of this traversal is the primary goal of tracing.

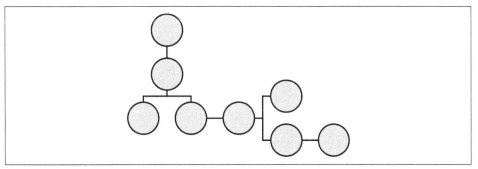

Figure 12-3. A tracing web. The purpose of distributed tracing is to understand where messages originate and terminate and where they go on their journey.

For us to better understand tracing, it's worth talking about interceptors. In Pulsar, interceptors run on the brokers and intercept messages coming into Pulsar or going out of Pulsar. Interceptors can be helpful for operations that strictly require message mutation before arriving at a consumer or a producer. The two most prominent use cases for interceptors are data validation and metadata addition. It's probably not hard to imagine a producer interceptor being used for schema validation. In this scenario, the producer publishes a message to Pulsar, and before the message is written to the topic, an interceptor ensures that it matches the registered schema. You may also imagine an interceptor tagging a message with metadata like a timestamp before sending it along (see Figure 12-4).

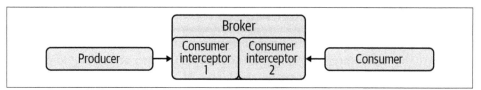

Figure 12-4. The interceptor framework in Apache Pulsar enables broker-side logic to be executed before arriving at the broker or consumer.

Tracing is the process of adding metadata to a payload to trace its progress through a system. Pulsar utilizes consumer and producer interceptors for its distributed tracing implementation by intercepting the messages with metadata and integrating with a tracing system like Jaeger or Skywalking.

In practice, an example may look like this:

```
Consumer<Double> consumer = client.newConsumer(Schema.Double)
        .topic("my-topic")
        .subscriptionName("my-sub")
        .subscriptionType(SubscriptionType.Shared)
        .intercept(new TracingConsumerInterceptor<>())
        .subscribe();

Producer<String> producerB = client.newProducer(Schema.STRING)
        .topic("my-topic-2")
        .intercept(new TracingProducerInterceptor())
        .create();
```

Pulsar SQL Metrics

Pulsar SQL can provide a rich interactive layer over Pulsar topics. Pulsar SQL utilizes Trino for SQL queries and is contingent on the types of queries run. Pulsar SQL can be resource intensive and may require additional resources to provide the best experience. Pulsar SQL provides a comprehensive set of metrics that are helpful in diagnosing problems as well as capacity planning (see Figure 12-5). Available metrics include the following:

split_bytes_read *(Counter)*
 This metric represents the number of bytes read from Apache BookKeeper.

split_num_messages_deserialized *(Counter)*
 This metric represents the number of messages deserialized by Pulsar SQL.

split_num_record_deserialized *(Counter)*
 This metric represents the number of records deserialized by Pulsar SQL.

split_bytes_read_per_query *(Summary)*
 This metric represents the number of bytes read per query.

split_entry_deserialize_time *(Summary)*
 This metric represents the total time spent deserializing table entries, measured in milliseconds.

split_entry_deserialize_time_per_query *(Summary)*
 This metric represents the time spent deserializing entries per query.

split_entry_queue_dequeue_wait_time *(Summary)*
 This metric represents the time spent waiting to get a new entry from the queue.

split_entry_queue_dequeue_wait_time_per_query *(Summary)*
 This metric represents the time spent waiting to get a new entry from the queue per query.

split_num_entries_per_batch *(Summary)*
 This metric represents the number of entries per batch.

split_num_entries_per_query *(Summary)*
 This metric represents the number of entries per query.

split_num_messages_deserialized_per_entry *(Summary)*
 This metric represents the number of messages that are deserialized per entry.

split_num_messages_deserialized_per_query *(Summary)*
 This metric represents the number of messages that are deserialized per query.

split_read_attempts *(Summary)*
 This metric represents the overall number of read attempts.

split_read_attempts_per_query *(Summary)*
 This metric represents the number of read attempts per query.

split_read_latency_per_batch *(Summary)*
 This metric represents the read latency per batch.

`split_read_latency_per_query` (*Summary*)
This metric represents the read latency per query.

`split_record_deserialize_time` (*Summary*)
This metric represents the time spent deserializing messages to records, measured in milliseconds.

`split_record_deserialize_time_per_query` (*Summary*)
This metric represents the total time spent deserializing messages per query.

`split_total_execution_time` (*Summary*)
This metric represents the total execution time for a given query.

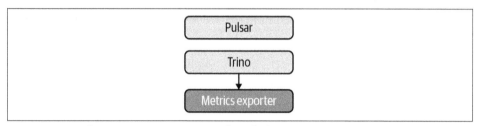

Figure 12-5. Pulsar SQL metrics are sent directly from Trino to the metrics exporter. These metrics can be used to detect performance issues and determine whether scaling up is necessary.

Metrics Forwarding

Pulsar's metrics are exposed via a `/metrics` endpoint in a format that works with time series databases such as Prometheus, InfluxDB, and TimescaleDB. Metrics can also be accessed by systems such as SignalFx, Datadog, and New Relic via these endpoints. Additionally, the value of forwarding the metrics to a time series database is the ability to visualize the metrics on a dashboard and set alerts for when the behavior of the metric is deviant from what we expect (see Figure 12-6). In the end, the value of collecting all the metrics we can about Pulsar is to understand its pathology and be able to diagnose when it's unhealthy—that is, to forward all metrics to a system where we can further analyze them and become good caretakers.

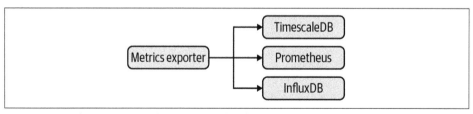

Figure 12-6. There are several time series database options on the market. Operators can choose other databases besides Prometheus and get the same rich experience.

Dashboards

The purpose of collecting all the metrics and forwarding them to a time series data-base is so that we can:

- Receive alerts based on anomalies
- Create dashboards to share with stakeholders and track performance

Grafana is a tool that is used to take metrics from a time series database like Prometheus and turn them into beautiful visualizations. Figure 12-7 provides an example of a Grafana dashboard.

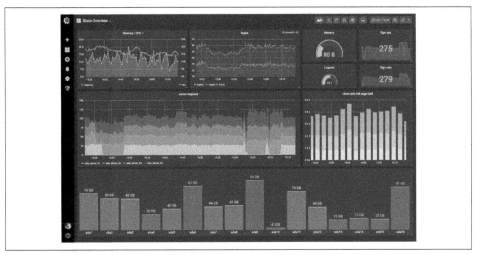

Figure 12-7. The Grafana dashboard utilizes summaries, gauges, histograms, and counters to visualize metrics from a time series database.

I've created some templates for Grafana that I'll share on my website (*http://www.jowanza.com/mastering-pulsar-content*) for anyone interested in creating dashboards for tracking Pulsar.

Summary

In this chapter we walked through available metrics for monitoring and operating Pulsar. With the conclusion of this chapter, we've covered the lion's share of topics in Pulsar and this is the end of the journey. In Chapter 13, I provide some of my thoughts on what the future of Pulsar might look like.

The Future

Pulsar began with the goal of being a general-purpose system for event streams and queues. Today the goals for Pulsar are more ambitious. Pulsar aims to be not just a messaging system, but a general-purpose storage engine and complete event platform. Pulsar also aims to support anyone on their streaming journey by supporting a proxy framework. What components are needed to make this ambitious goal a reality? This chapter isn't a comprehensive look at Pulsar's future; instead, it's my opinion of the areas worth tackling next. My opinions are colored by my experience building systems that use Pulsar or similar technology.

Programming Language Support

Pulsar has support for Java, Python, and Go officially, with many unofficial clients for other programming languages provided by the community. *Official* language support means that the Pulsar open source project maintains the implementation for that client. Pulsar's adoption in the broader ecosystem hinges partially on its ability to reach programmers with whatever tools they are comfortable with. Language support extends beyond client libraries to Pulsar Functions and even Pulsar IO implementations. Supporting the top 25 most popular programming languages is an undertaking that shouldn't be placed solely on the shoulders of Pulsar source contributors. Providing a native, language-specific implementation is a time-consuming ordeal and not necessarily a core function of Pulsar. With these limitations, how should Pulsar expand its reach and support for more programming languages? An improved approach is building a native implementation of the Pulsar client wrapped via a foreign function interface (FFI) and implemented across the board.

Extension Interface

The Python implementation of the Pulsar client library utilizes a shared native implementation of the Pulsar client. This native implementation enables the Python client to have parity in performance with the Java client and keep in lockstep with the client without reimplementation (see Figure 13-1). This model for building client libraries is similar to other client library implementations for databases, message queues, and other driver-based software.[1] Many of these systems have needs that make them good candidates for using the interface pattern.

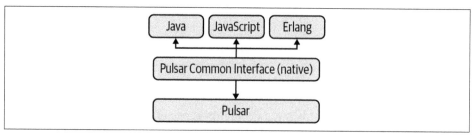

Figure 13-1. The Pulsar Common Interface is a C codebase enabling language extension via foreign function interfaces.

First, each of these driver-based software implementations has performance requirements. We expect our database to return data quickly, our message queue to receive data at imperceptible speeds, and our printer to receive our print job quickly. Second, we expect these implementations to be efficient. We want to run with as few resources as possible and maybe in constrained environments like an A/V system. Third, we want these systems to run in as many places as possible. We want polyglot implementations of our database and message clients, and we want our printers to work on Macs, Windows, and Linux. To accomplish this, a native implementation is often required (one written in C or C++).

An excellent native client library implementation enables other programming languages to tap into their ecosystems to provide a performant and idiomatically acceptable implementation. In the long term, I see all Pulsar client libraries developed using this pattern.

Enhancements to Pulsar Functions

Pulsar Functions provide a simple programmatic interface for stream processing in Pulsar. The beauty of Pulsar Functions is their simplicity, small runtime, and flexible scale-out model. Pulsar Functions are not suitable for every stream processing problem, only those that involve complex state management. I don't think it's wise for

---

1 Apache Kafka, RabbitMQ, and Redis are some examples of open source projects that take this approach.

Pulsar Functions to build the same capabilities of a stream processing framework as Apache Flink. Still, I do think a few extensions might improve the usability for complex use cases.

Watermarks

Stream processing systems are concerned with processing messages quickly. However, they are also concerned with correctness. Correctness means the data processed by the stream processing engine reflects the state of the real world. A discrepancy might arise when the stream processing system is late or out of order. Consider a stream processing application that sums the count of events every 10 seconds to provide a rolling count. If events arrive outside of that 10-second window, the stream processing system is attributing the count to messages that arrived late but belonged to an earlier window (see Figure 13-2).

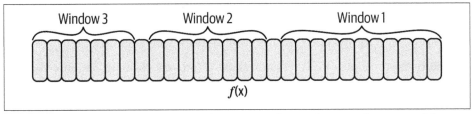

Figure 13-2. Windows over an immutable stream. The windows are finite sets of elements that can be determined by code.

To deal with the issue of late-arriving data, stream processing engines have a concept known as watermarks. Watermarks allow the stream processing engine to deal with its timer and the time in the events and then deal with late-arriving data. I think Pulsar Functions should include some notion of optional watermarks. I think it would allow for richer interactions and support use cases that would traditionally go to a system like Apache Flink.

Windowing

Pulsar Functions support windowing via the Java SDK. Windows allow you to perform a stream processing task on a finite set of data bounded by time (see Figure 13-3). My only improvement suggestion for the future of Pulsar is to extend this functionality to the other programming languages in the Pulsar Functions ecosystem. Enabling this kind of capability across all languages creates a polyglot utopia of sorts where all programmers can be introduced to ideas of stream processing in a friendly and inviting environment.

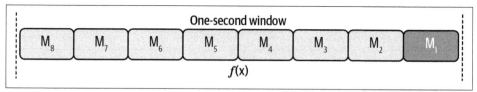

One-second window

| M_8 | M_7 | M_6 | M_5 | M_4 | M_3 | M_2 | M_1 |

$f(x)$

Figure 13-3. A time-based window on a one-second interval. Messages M_1–M_8 would be processed by the window function.

Complex event processing

Complex event processing (CEP) is a subset of event processing that builds complex state machines from stream processing jobs. A large amount of business logic may be required to execute some event pipelines. This logic may include many failure and retry conditions, circuit breakers, and other complex behaviors. Utilizing higher-level event processing APIs for this task can be cumbersome and error prone. CEP APIs try to pull the complexity away from the user and provide an abstraction with built-in mechanisms for retry and other required behaviors for fault tolerance.

To solidify the concept of CEP, let's talk about a concrete example. Suppose you are creating a home security system. In a home security system, there are sensors (window, door, glass break) and these sensors help provide a state of the home. As the home security company, you can search for anomalies in the state of the sensors to determine whether something is wrong. For example, if it's late at night and glass breaks, then maybe it was a burglary. Within a home, there are many complex interactions and reasons for sensors to be in different states (see Figure 13-4), so it may be advantageous to look at events in conjunction with each other to determine where the anomalies are. Wherever there are complex patterns in event streaming systems is where CEP thrives.

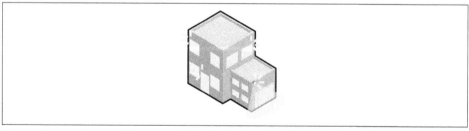

Figure 13-4. A home with sensors. Windows, doors, and the camera all have sensors and in conjunction lead to the home being in different states that can be monitored by the security company.

Apache Flink is a system I've mentioned a few times in this book. Flink has a robust set of CEP APIs to find patterns in streams. For example, if you wanted to check a stream for an event happening two or more times, it would be represented like this:

```
start.timesOrMore(2);
```

We could use patterns like this to build a rudimentary system for monitoring a home (see Figure 13-5) and get much more sophisticated in time.

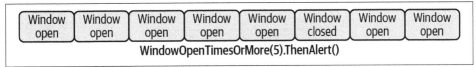

Figure 13-5. Going from right to left, we see five "window open" events which would trigger an alert.

More than simple pattern matching, Flink also supports logical operators like `where` and `or` in the CEP API:

```
pattern.where(new SimpleCondition<Event>() {
    @Override
    public boolean filter(Event value) {
        return true
    }
}).or(new SimpleCondition<Event>() {
    @Override
    public boolean filter(Event value) {
        return false
    }
});
```

It is possible to represent this kind of logic with Pulsar Functions, but it would be difficult and might vary from implementation to implementation. As I mentioned throughout this book, one of the notable features of Pulsar Functions is their simplicity. I think some of the pattern matching used in CEP would be a welcome addition, but all of it would be too much to adopt.

WebAssembly (WASM)

So far in this chapter we've focused on Pulsar interoperability. Similar to the Pulsar client, Pulsar Functions should be extended to every programming language. Chapter 7 talked in depth about Pulsar Functions and how complex it is to create runtimes for different languages. Performing the same exercise across multiple programming languages would take a lifetime of effort. Instead of approaching it piecemeal, Pulsar can utilize a similar approach to a native client library.

WebAssembly (WASM) is an efficient binary instruction format and a suitable compilation target for any language. This means any programming language should be able to compile to WebAssembly. If the Pulsar Functions runtime were changed to a WASM runtime, any programming language with a WASM target could write a Pulsar function (see Figure 13-6). The implications for this change are massive. Not only would Pulsar Functions benefit from the performance gains of WASM, but Pulsar Functions would be language agnostic. I should note that WASM is in its infancy and not every language supports it as a compilation target. That said, there is plenty of momentum around it, and other streaming technology platforms have adopted it for specific workloads (*https://oreil.ly/Zdukb*).

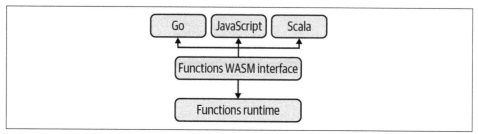

Figure 13-6. Pulsar Functions can be written in many native implementations, and can be compiled to a common WASM runtime and run as Pulsar Functions.

Architectural Simplification/Expansion

One unfair criticism you'll find in reviews of Apache Pulsar is that the architecture and deployment are too complex. Throughout this book, I've shown how every decision in Pulsar is carefully considered and every component of the system serves a well-defined purpose. That said, as the Pulsar ecosystem evolves and use cases continue to expand, some modularity in Pulsar will be welcome. Two examples are Pulsar's metadata management and append-only log implementation.

Metadata management

In a Pulsar deployment, Apache ZooKeeper is where the lion's share of metadata is stored. ZooKeeper is purpose built for storing metadata. However, ZooKeeper is a dependency that requires attention on behalf of its operators. While Pulsar is inextricably linked to ZooKeeper today, there may be good reasons to move away from utilizing ZooKeeper in the future.

In Chapter 4 we talked a little bit about Kafka's move away from utilizing ZooKeeper and moving metadata management and its consensus algorithm to the Kafka brokers themselves. As Confluent (a maintainer of Kafka) noted in an article (*https://oreil.ly/hAMNC*), removing ZooKeeper simplified the development process of Kafka and allowed Kafka to go in a different direction for the future of the project. Pulsar utilizes ZooKeeper in some of the same ways that Kafka did, and there may be some benefit from going in a similar direction (see Figure 13-7).

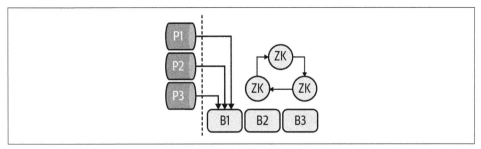

Figure 13-7. In this scenario, Pulsar manages its own metadata to keep track of ledgers and communicates with BookKeeper.

The goals of Pulsar are modularity, user choice, and configurability. Instead of removing ZooKeeper altogether, the Pulsar maintainers may provide an API that can allow the Pulsar operator to use other systems to store metadata and configurations. Systems like HashiCorp Consul, ETCD, and distributed key–value databases may all be good options for storing metadata for Pulsar (see Figure 13-8).

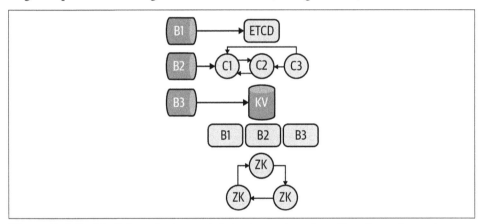

Figure 13-8. In this Pulsar cluster, metadata storage is replaced by alternative systems like ETCD, HashiCorp Consul, and a key–value database.

Log expansion

In Chapter 5, we talked in depth about Apache BookKeeper. BookKeeper provides the storage mechanism for Pulsar topics, Pulsar Functions' state, and other data necessary for operating a Pulsar cluster. Utilizing BookKeeper for data storage and retrieval has been successful for Pulsar; however, new implementations might enable new deployment topologies and use cases.

We know that BookKeeper's implementation of a distributed log is reliable, scalable, and relatively easy to deploy on cloud native platforms, so why would Pulsar ever want to get rid of it? The only reasonable answer to that question is if an even *better*

ZooKeeper came along; that is, a new implementation of a distributed log that was faster, more scalable, and cheaper to operate. At this point, it's an academic exercise, but should the day come when the interface between Pulsar and BookKeeper is well defined and modular, moving to that better ZooKeeper wouldn't be a stretch or overly burdensome.

Messaging Platform Bridges

One mechanism that aids in Pulsar adoption is Pulsar bridges. The three most popular bridges are Kafka-on-Pulsar (see Figure 13-9), MQTT-on-Pulsar (see Figure 13-10), and AMQP-on-Pulsar[2] (see Figure 13-11).

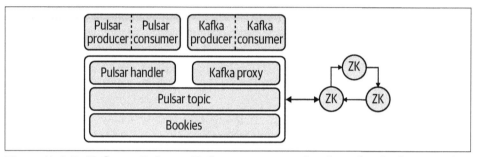

Figure 13-9. In Kafka-on-Pulsar, a Kafka proxy runs within the Pulsar broker to enable communication with the Kafka protocol without interfering with the existing Pulsar communication.

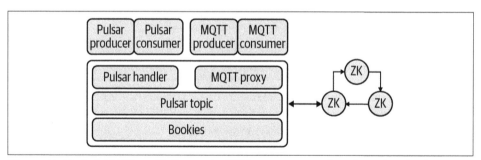

Figure 13-10. In MQTT-on-Kafka, an MQTT proxy runs within the Pulsar broker to enable communication with the MQTT protocol without impacting Pulsar clients communicating with the broker.

---

2 AMQP 0.9.1 Protocol, and not AMP 1.0 Protocol.

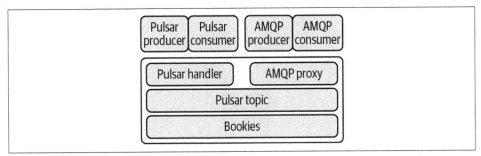

Figure 13-11. In AMQP-on-Pulsar, the Pulsar broker runs an AMQP protocol proxy so that traffic from AMQP 0.9.1 clients can communicate with the Pulsar cluster without interfering with existing Pulsar protocol traffic.

These bridges enable the user to use Kafka, AMQP 0.9.1, or MQTT, and messages are translated into the Pulsar protocol. Platform bridges ease transitions from other message platforms to Pulsar. They also provide a mechanism for users to try their existing system and Pulsar in conjunction. In addition to the bridges provided today, there is some room for expanding these bridges in Pulsar.

The purpose of the bridges is not only to increase the adoption of Pulsar, but with Pulsar's storage model, they also allow users to enjoy both systems and leverage them for their semantics. Two places where I see value for platform bridges are with NATS and AMQP 1.0 Protocol.

NATS

NATS is a popular messaging system focused on lightweight and edge deployments. The core NATS protocol does not have a concept of event streams. However, NATS has a subproject called JetStream (*https://oreil.ly/kpp3y*) that does include an event streams implementation. Where NATS excels is in resource-constrained environments and at the edge where bandwidth for the protocol has a considerable impact on performance. NATS JetStream implementation has some similar limitations to other event streaming systems because it doesn't separate the storage and compute parts of its platform (see Figure 13-12).

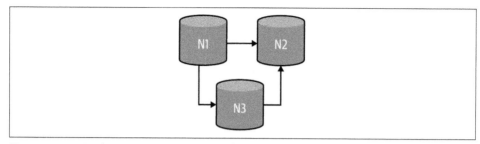

Figure 13-12. In this NATS JetStream topology, NATS brokers are stateful (each broker has some responsibility for the topics stored in NATS, including storing the data).

A NATS-on-Pulsar bridge would allow NATS to continue to excel at what it does best while enabling access to the greater Pulsar ecosystem and storage primitives (see Figure 13-13).

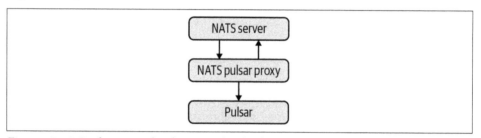

Figure 13-13. In this example of a NATS bridge for Pulsar, the NATS protocol is translated to and from the Pulsar protocol. Messages are stored in Pulsar, but only the NATS protocol is accessible from this message path.

AMQP 1.0

Advanced Message Queuing Protocol (AMQP) 1.0 is an open protocol for messages and exchanges. AMQP 1.0 implementations span both open source and proprietary message brokers. AMQP 1.0 is the default protocol for Microsoft Azure messaging systems and for ActiveMQ Artemis. Currently, AMQP 1.0 does not have a concept of event streams[3] as part of the protocol, making it a good bridge for Pulsar. An AMQP 1.0 Pulsar bridge would enable workloads on ActiveMQ to have some long-term storage and additional failover modes (see Figure 13-14).

---

3 Oasis Open, the foundation that oversees the AMQP 1.0 Protocol, is actively working on adding an event stream concept to the protocol (*https://oreil.ly/c5OAY*).

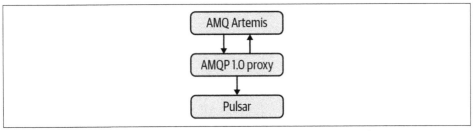

Figure 13-14. In this example, workloads that traditionally are hosted on ActiveMQ Artemis can be ported to Pulsar.

Summary

In this book you learned about Apache Pulsar, not only about its components but also the ecosystem that has emerged as a consequence of its success. As a project, Pulsar has pushed the industry forward. I would summarize the most impactful ideas in Pulsar as follows:

- Separating the concerns of storage from the messaging system
- A distributed log as the base implementation for storage

Pulsar separates the needs of storage from the other needs in the messaging system. This decision makes Pulsar more fault tolerant as a node in a Pulsar cluster can fail and the responsibilities of that node will move to another in the cluster. This design decision has wide-reaching implications, including making it easier to support tiered storage.

In Chapter 2 we talked about the novelty of the distributed log. With Pulsar, it's a distributed log "all the way down," meaning that not only are topics stored in a distributed log, but metadata about the cluster and storage for cursors is stored there as well. Pulsar's distributed log implementation is unique and sets it apart from others in the field. It's why I was able to spend the pages of this book expounding on the ecosystem and the tooling in Pulsar.

In 2021, Pulsar is a project that is growing in popularity, as companies big and small are adopting it and contributing to the open source project. Several companies are packaging the open source project with value-added services and creating thriving businesses. The future is bright for Pulsar, but the ecosystem will continue to evolve to meet the needs of this community. It's been a pleasure to spend a year writing this book, getting to know members of the community, and becoming intimately familiar with Pulsar. I've spent countless hours looking at code, reading articles, and determining the best way to share this project. I hope this book can serve as a reference guide for those who are familiar with Pulsar, and I hope that it serves as a great introduction to newcomers.

Pulsar Admin API

Throughout the book, I've used the Pulsar Admin REST API to perform many tasks. I shared the URLs and the API methods but didn't spend much time talking about the REST API. That was partly due to it not fitting into the flow of the book, but also knowing I would reserve this section of the book to talk about it. This appendix will quickly cover the Pulsar Admin API and go through all the available methods in the API. It's here to serve as a reference (see Table A-1).

For an exhaustive list of what is available in the Pulsar Admin API, you can consult the official API reference (*https://oreil.ly/U4Wml*).

Table A-1. Available methods on the Pulsar Admin API

Object	Methods
Bookies	Methods for getting information about currently running bookies as well as editing and deleting metadata about running bookies
Broker-Stats	Methods for retrieving statistics about brokers in the cluster
Brokers	Methods for getting, deleting, and setting broker-level configurations
Clusters	Methods for getting, deleting, and setting cluster-level configurations
Namespaces	Methods for getting, deleting, creating, and setting namespaces
Nonpersistent topic	Methods for retrieving information on nonpersistent topics as well as creating and editing them
Persistent topic	Methods for retrieving information on persistent topics as well as creating and editing them
Resource-Quotas	Methods for retrieving and setting resource quotas
ResourceGroups	Methods for getting, creating, and deleting resource groups
Schemas	Methods for retrieving, creating, editing, and deleting schemas
Tenants	Methods for retrieving, creating, editing, and deleting tenants

Use Cases

The Pulsar Admin API can perform any function that would require using the CLI, but can do so via RESTful semantics. REST APIs can be more easily exposed to the internet and are useful for automation, auditing, and building integrations. Following are some useful things that have been done with the Pulsar Admin API:

Billing integration

In a company I worked at previously, we collected usage statistics from the metrics API as well as metadata from the REST API to create a dashboard for usage of our Pulsar cluster. This dashboard showed us estimated costs per topic based on our cloud costs and usage in the cluster.

Topic creation

I've used the REST API to ensure that topics were only created by authorized parties and in the correct semantics. As part of a merge request, developers needed to include the REST command used to create their topic, and we validated it before approving the merge request. Additionally, our automated CI/CD system would run the REST command and check it for correctness.

Auditing

At a previous company, we got started using the Pulsar Admin CLI and did not have any tight controls on administration. After some time, we needed to audit what was out there and we used the Pulsar Admin API to generate lists of topics and their metadata as well as other resources. We were able to use this list to form policies and enforce them going forward.

Examples

Here are a few examples of using the Pulsar Admin REST API to perform some useful work in a cluster. It's not an exhaustive list, but just intended to give you an idea of how the API bodies and methods work.

Creating a Partitioned Topic

This command creates a partitioned topic with 10 partitions:

```
PUT https://pulsar.apache.org/admin/v2/non-persistent/
  {tenant}/{namespace}/{topic}/partitions
-body 10
```

Deleting a Partitioned Topic

This command will force the deletion of a nonpersistent and partitioned topic:

```
DELETE https://pulsar.apache.org/admin/v2/non-persistent/
  {tenant}/{namespace}/{topic}/partitions?force=true
```

Creating a Namespace with Specific Policies

With this command you can set every possible configuration for a namespace. You'll notice many of the values look familiar, as we've used them throughout the book. You can even set arbitrary properties which can be useful for tracking company-specific information about a namespace:

```
PUT https://pulsar.apache.org/admin/v2/namespaces/{tenant}/{namespace}
```

Body

```
{
  "auth_policies": {
    "topicAuthentication": {
      "property1": {
        "property1": [
          "produce"
        ],
        "property2": [
          "produce"
        ]
      },
      "property2": {
        "property1": [
          "produce"
        ],
        "property2": [
          "produce"
        ]
      }
    },
    "subscriptionAuthentication": {
      "property1": [
        "string"
      ],
      "property2": [
        "string"
      ]
    },
    "namespaceAuthentication": {
      "property1": [
        "produce"
      ],
      "property2": [
        "produce"
      ]
    }
  },
  "replication_clusters": [
```

```
      "string"
    ],
    "bundles": {
      "boundaries": [
        "string"
      ],
      "numBundles": 0
    },
    "backlog_quota_map": {
      "property1": {
        "limitSize": 0,
        "limitTime": 0,
        "policy": "producer_request_hold"
      },
      "property2": {
        "limitSize": 0,
        "limitTime": 0,
        "policy": "producer_request_hold"
      }
    },
    "clusterDispatchRate": {
      "property1": {
        "dispatchThrottlingRateInMsg": 0,
        "dispatchThrottlingRateInByte": 0,
        "relativeToPublishRate": true,
        "ratePeriodInSecond": 0
      },
      "property2": {
        "dispatchThrottlingRateInMsg": 0,
        "dispatchThrottlingRateInByte": 0,
        "relativeToPublishRate": true,
        "ratePeriodInSecond": 0
      }
    },
    "topicDispatchRate": {
      "property1": {
        "dispatchThrottlingRateInMsg": 0,
        "dispatchThrottlingRateInByte": 0,
        "relativeToPublishRate": true,
        "ratePeriodInSecond": 0
      },
      "property2": {
        "dispatchThrottlingRateInMsg": 0,
        "dispatchThrottlingRateInByte": 0,
        "relativeToPublishRate": true,
        "ratePeriodInSecond": 0
      }
    },
    "subscriptionDispatchRate": {
      "property1": {
        "dispatchThrottlingRateInMsg": 0,
        "dispatchThrottlingRateInByte": 0,
```

```json
      "relativeToPublishRate": true,
      "ratePeriodInSecond": 0
  },
  "property2": {
    "dispatchThrottlingRateInMsg": 0,
    "dispatchThrottlingRateInByte": 0,
    "relativeToPublishRate": true,
    "ratePeriodInSecond": 0
  }
},
"replicatorDispatchRate": {
  "property1": {
    "dispatchThrottlingRateInMsg": 0,
    "dispatchThrottlingRateInByte": 0,
    "relativeToPublishRate": true,
    "ratePeriodInSecond": 0
  },
  "property2": {
    "dispatchThrottlingRateInMsg": 0,
    "dispatchThrottlingRateInByte": 0,
    "relativeToPublishRate": true,
    "ratePeriodInSecond": 0
  }
},
"clusterSubscribeRate": {
  "property1": {
    "subscribeThrottlingRatePerConsumer": 0,
    "ratePeriodInSecond": 0
  },
  "property2": {
    "subscribeThrottlingRatePerConsumer": 0,
    "ratePeriodInSecond": 0
  }
},
"persistence": {
  "bookkeeperEnsemble": 0,
  "bookkeeperWriteQuorum": 0,
  "bookkeeperAckQuorum": 0,
  "managedLedgerMaxMarkDeleteRate": 0
},
"deduplicationEnabled": true,
"autoTopicCreationOverride": {
  "topicType": "string",
  "defaultNumPartitions": 0,
  "allowAutoTopicCreation": true
},
"autoSubscriptionCreationOverride": {
  "allowAutoSubscriptionCreation": true
},
"publishMaxMessageRate": {
  "property1": {
    "publishThrottlingRateInMsg": 0,
```

```
      "publishThrottlingRateInByte": 0
    },
    "property2": {
      "publishThrottlingRateInMsg": 0,
      "publishThrottlingRateInByte": 0
    }
  },
  "latency_stats_sample_rate": {
    "property1": 0,
    "property2": 0
  },
  "message_ttl_in_seconds": 0,
  "subscription_expiration_time_minutes": 0,
  "retention_policies": {
    "retentionTimeInMinutes": 0,
    "retentionSizeInMB": 0
  },
  "deleted": true,
  "encryption_required": true,
  "delayed_delivery_policies": {
    "tickTime": 0,
    "active": true
  },
  "inactive_topic_policies": {
    "inactiveTopicDeleteMode": "delete_when_no_subscriptions",
    "maxInactiveDurationSeconds": 0,
    "deleteWhileInactive": true
  },
  "subscription_auth_mode": "None",
  "max_producers_per_topic": 0,
  "max_consumers_per_topic": 0,
  "max_consumers_per_subscription": 0,
  "max_unacked_messages_per_consumer": 0,
  "max_unacked_messages_per_subscription": 0,
  "max_subscriptions_per_topic": 0,
  "compaction_threshold": 0,
  "offload_threshold": 0,
  "offload_deletion_lag_ms": 0,
  "max_topics_per_namespace": 0,
  "schema_auto_update_compatibility_strategy": "AutoUpdateDisabled",
  "schema_compatibility_strategy": "UNDEFINED",
  "is_allow_auto_update_schema": true,
  "schema_validation_enforced": true,
  "offload_policies": {
    "managedLedgerOffloadPrefetchRounds": 0,
    "s3ManagedLedgerOffloadRegion": "string",
    "s3ManagedLedgerOffloadBucket": "string",
    "s3ManagedLedgerOffloadServiceEndpoint": "string",
    "s3ManagedLedgerOffloadMaxBlockSizeInBytes": 0,
    "s3ManagedLedgerOffloadReadBufferSizeInBytes": 0,
    "s3ManagedLedgerOffloadCredentialId": "string",
    "s3ManagedLedgerOffloadCredentialSecret": "string",
```

```
    "s3ManagedLedgerOffloadRole": "string",
    "s3ManagedLedgerOffloadRoleSessionName": "string",
    "gcsManagedLedgerOffloadRegion": "string",
    "gcsManagedLedgerOffloadBucket": "string",
    "gcsManagedLedgerOffloadMaxBlockSizeInBytes": 0,
    "gcsManagedLedgerOffloadReadBufferSizeInBytes": 0,
    "gcsManagedLedgerOffloadServiceAccountKeyFile": "string",
    "fileSystemProfilePath": "string",
    "fileSystemURI": "string",
    "managedLedgerOffloadBucket": "string",
    "managedLedgerOffloadedReadPriority": "BOOKKEEPER_FIRST",
    "managedLedgerOffloadRegion": "string",
    "managedLedgerOffloadServiceEndpoint": "string",
    "managedLedgerOffloadMaxBlockSizeInBytes": 0,
    "managedLedgerOffloadReadBufferSizeInBytes": 0,
    "managedLedgerOffloadThresholdInBytes": 0,
    "managedLedgerOffloadDeletionLagInMillis": 0,
    "managedLedgerOffloadDriver": "string",
    "offloadersDirectory": "string",
    "managedLedgerOffloadMaxThreads": 0
  },
  "deduplicationSnapshotIntervalSeconds": 0,
  "subscription_types_enabled": [
    "string"
  ],
  "properties": {
    "property1": "string",
    "property2": "string"
  },
  "resource_group_name": "string"
}
```

Deleting a Namespace

This command will delete a namespace and all the topics in that namespace (use with caution):

```
DELETE https://pulsar.apache.org/admin/v2/namespaces/{tenant}/{namespace}
```

Summary

Pulsar has an undeniably rich REST Admin API. As an operator of Pulsar, you can perform any task you need to from the REST Admin API. However, with great power comes great responsibility. Before running Pulsar at scale and using the Admin API, it's recommended that you spend some time familiarizing yourself with what the API is capable of as well as what it means. You should also follow authorization best practices to prevent someone from using the REST Admin API to do irreversible damage in the cluster.

Pulsar Admin CLI

Throughout the book, I've used the Pulsar Admin CLI to perform many tasks. I shared snippets of the commands but didn't really dive into the bigger picture of the CLI. That was partly due to it not fitting into the flow of the book, but also due to knowing I would reserve this section of the book to talk about it. This appendix will quickly cover the Pulsar Admin CLI and go through all of the resources available on the CLI. It's here to serve as a reference (see Table B-1).

For an exhaustive list of what is available in the Pulsar Admin CLI, you can consult the official CLI reference (*https://oreil.ly/4GOt9*).

Table B-1. Available resources on the Pulsar Admin CLI

Resource	Purpose
Brokers	List, delete, and edit brokers and metadata about brokers
Broker-stats	Retrieve broker statistics
Clusters	List, delete, and edit clusters and metadata about clusters
Functions	List, create, delete, and edit Pulsar Functions and metadata
Namespaces	List, create, delete, and edit Pulsar namespaces
ns-isolation-policy	Manage Pulsar namespace isolation policies
Sources	List, create, delete, and edit Pulsar IO sources
Sinks	List, create, delete, and edit Pulsar IO sinks
Topics	List, create, delete, and edit Pulsar topics
Tenants	List, create, delete, and edit Pulsar tenants
Resource-quotas	Manage Pulsar resource-quotas
Schemas	List and manage schemas used in the schema registry
Packages	Manage packaged versions used throughout Pulsar

CLI API

The CLI API is consistent across all the resources in the Pulsar Admin API. This makes it easy to remember and also easy to reason about if you don't know the exact command for the CLI. The format is:

```
$ pulsar-admin <resource> <subcommand>
```

For each resource, you can find hints by asking for help on that specific resource:

```
$ pulsar-admin <resource> -h
```

Let's look at a few examples of this in action.

Examples

In this section, I'll share a few commands for performing common tasks with the Pulsar CLI.

Creating a Partitioned Topic

This command creates a partitioned topic with 100 partitions:

```
$ pulsar-admin topics create-partitioned-topic -p 100
```

Creating a Pulsar IO Source

This command creates a Pulsar IO source. Options include picking a source and sharing configuration files with Pulsar:

```
$ pulsar-admin sources create options
```

Creating a Pulsar IO Sink

This command creates a Pulsar IO sink. Options include picking a sink and sharing configuration files with Pulsar:

```
$ pulsar-admin sinks create options
```

Uploading a Schema

This command uploads a schema to the schema registry with the schema definition provided by the file:

```
$ pulsar-admin schemas upload -f myschema.json
```

Deleting a Schema

This command deletes a specific schema:

```
$ pulsar-admin schemas delete options
```

Creating a Namespace

This command creates a namespace with specified options. Options include clusters in which to enable the new namespace:

```
$ pulsar-admin namespaces create options
```

Deleting a Namespace

This command deletes a namespace with options:

```
$ pulsar-admin namespaces delete options
```

Summary

As you can see, the Pulsar Admin CLI is a powerful tool. Similar to the REST API, we can perform all the necessary administrative tasks with the Pulsar Admin CLI. It's important to remember that access to full CLI capabilities should be restricted to staff who have experience, and operations like deleting should be carefully considered.

Geo-Replication

Geo-replication is the process of replicating (copying) data across multiple regions or multiple datacenters. I didn't talk much about geo-replication in the book because there is a considerable amount to cover on Pulsar and fitting this in was hard. I decided to include it in this appendix because I still feel it's important. Typically, geo-replication has one of two motivating factors:

- Preparation for disaster recovery scenarios
- Localizing data or making global data available everywhere

Applications that run on the internet are subjected to many conditions by which they can fail. Applications run on physical hardware that sits in a datacenter. Datacenters[1] can lose power, lose connectivity to the internet, be flooded, or have their hardware fail. The way datacenters combat these problems is by enabling applications to run across multiple datacenters (regions), or multiple places within a datacenter (availability zones). The datacenter can guarantee some level of reliability for each zone and also each region. By spreading your application across regions and zones, you can decrease the likelihood that you will encounter a failure that results in your applications being unavailable.

Many companies that start on the internet start by serving one geographic audience. Typically, it is the audience in the country of their founding. As the company gains traction and looks to expand its footprint, it may open offices and offer its product outside its home country. Oftentimes, this expansion requires deploying the application in a local cloud environment to reduce latency for new customers. This physical split of the application between countries can have some lasting consequences for the

---

1 When I say "datacenters" I mean either the public cloud or private datacenters.

company. In order to get a global view of what's happening with its data, it may have to do expensive, cross-datacenter replication. What can be done about this?

Geo-replication in Pulsar is built to address these problems directly when it comes to storing data in Pulsar. In this appendix I'll talk briefly about how geo-replication works and how to get started with it in Pulsar.

Synchronous Replication

In synchronous replication, each cluster has its own brokers, geographically distributed bookies, and a proxy, but all share a geographically distributed ZooKeeper cluster (see Figure C-1). This is because the managed ledger (a mapping of topics and where they are stored) is kept in ZooKeeper.

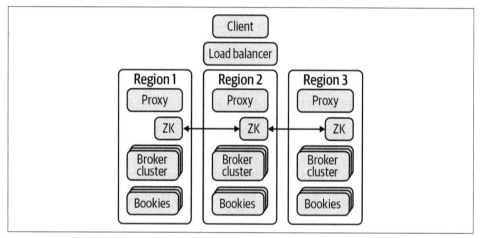

Figure C-1. In this synchronous replication setup, the bookies are shared across regions and ZooKeeper manages the ledgers. All writes will wait until acknowledgment from BookKeeper is received.

One thing you may notice about this replication setup is that every write requires full sync and replication across the bookies. As you can imagine, that can be a slower operation and round-trip latency can suffer. That said, consistency across all regions will be strong.

Asynchronous Replication

In asynchronous replication, each cluster manages its own resources (bookies, ZooKeeper instances, and brokers), but the brokers communicate with one another to determine where to replicate their data. One important difference is that the brokers can write data to their local instance of BookKeeper before replicating it to the other brokers (see Figure C-2). This makes for a faster operation but eventually an inherently more consistent state.

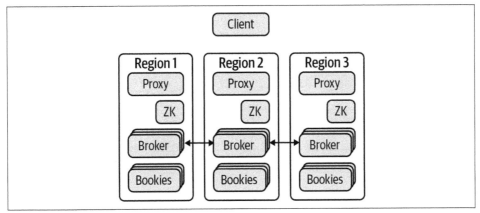

Figure C-2. In this example of asynchronous replication across Pulsar clusters, the brokers manage communication for syncing data across regions, making for a faster but more asynchronous experience.

Table C-1 provides a summary of the differences between the two replication approaches.

Table C-1. Comparing async and sync approaches to replication in Pulsar

	Async	Sync
ZooKeeper	Region	Global
BookKeeper	Region	Global
Brokers	Region	Region
Sync mechanism	Broker to broker	BookKeeper
Consistency	Eventual	Strong

Replication Patterns

There are many ways to configure your cluster for replication. This section covers some of the more popular ones:

- Mesh
- Aggregation
- Standby
- Producer side

Mesh

What most people think of with replication is synchronous replication, where every cluster has the same data as other clusters in the topology. In this method, clients can simply produce or consume from the closest geographic cluster and know their messages will be available to anyone in the cluster (see Figure C-3).

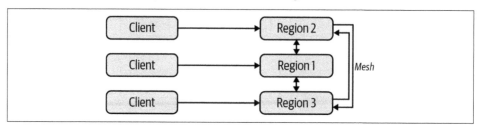

Figure C-3. In this mesh replication architecture, clients publish and consume from their nearest broker and replication is managed internally. Clients expect to always get a global state of the data within a time window.

As discussed earlier, a mesh would be best accomplished with a synchronous approach to replication. You can expect some amount of read latency that you can measure with the metrics you learned about in Chapter 12.

Aggregation

For some cases, replication is about providing a combined view of several clusters. For many who work in data engineering, ETL is often the process of taking data from various sources and combining it into a single view. A company using Pulsar may have several independent clusters that serve specific geographic locations or use cases, but may need to replicate the data to a centralized Pulsar cluster for aggregated views and analytics. You can have independent clusters and route all of their data to a specific cluster (see Figure C-4).

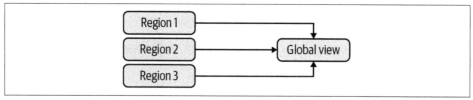

Figure C-4. Regions operate independent Pulsar clusters but replicate their data to a central cluster for a global view.

Setting up this kind of aggregation can be managed by setting namespace- and cluster-level policies with the Admin API or Admin CLI:

```
/pulsar/bin/pulsar-admin tenants create E-payments \ #A
--allowed-clusters us-west,us-east,us-central,internal
/pulsar/bin/pulsar-admin namespaces create E-payments/us-east-payments #B
/pulsar/bin/pulsar-admin namespaces create E-payments/us-west-payments
/pulsar/bin/pulsar-admin namespaces create E-payments/us-central-payments
/pulsar/bin/pulsar-admin namespaces set-clusters \ #C
E-payments/us-east-payments --clusters us-east,internal
/pulsar/bin/pulsar-admin namespaces set-clusters \ #D
E-payments/us-west-payments --clusters us-west,internal
/pulsar/bin/pulsar-admin namespaces set-clusters \ #E
E-payments/us-central-payments --clusters us-central,internal
```

Standby

So far, we've talked about cases where every cluster needs to receive data from the client. From a purely disaster recovery scenario, it is not needed or desired to have clients communicate with both clusters. For this scenario, we need one active cluster that is communicating with clients and another cluster in another region that is simply receiving and storing replicated data. A load balancer can be configured to accept traffic on the active cluster, and then Pulsar brokers can replicate data (either synchronously or asynchronously). In the event of a disaster, the standby cluster has most (in the async case) or all (in the sync case) of the data, and simply routing to the standby cluster and making it active will avert the disaster (see Figure C-5).

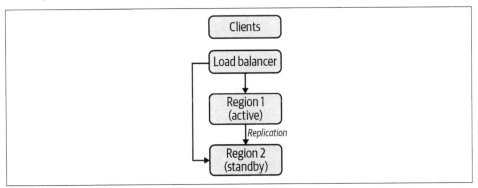

Figure C-5. An active cluster receiving messages from clients through a load balancer. In the case of a failure, the load balancer can route traffic to the standby cluster.

Admin- and Producer-Level Control

For one final note on geo-replication, let's talk about how administrators and producers can control which namespaces and topics are replicated.

From the administrator side, we can determine which regions are part of our namespace:

```
$ /pulsar/bin/pulsar-admin namespaces set-clusters
my-name-space --clusters us-east,us-west,turkey
```

In this command, I set my-name-space and assigned it to clusters located in us-east, us-west, and turkey. This gives me fine-grained control. Perhaps I don't want to replicate every topic globally, or maybe there are laws forbidding data from leaving a certain geographic region.

From the producer level, I can also use my knowledge of available datacenters to restrict certain messages from going to a specific region. I can do so with the client library:

```
List<String> myDataCenterList = Lists.newArrayList("us-west", "us-east");
Message message = MessageBuilder.create()
.setReplicationClusters(myDataCenterList)
.build();
producer.send(message);
```

As someone who has worked with geo-replication in other technologies, I find it impressive that Pulsar gives you geo-replication control all the way down to the client (see Figure C-6).

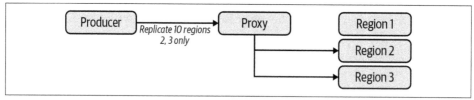

Figure C-6. In this example, the producer chooses to replicate the message only to Regions 2 and 3. Region 1 does not get the message.

Summary

Apache Pulsar supports geo-replication via synchronous and asynchronous methods. Geo-replication is helpful for disaster recovery as well as building applications that share a global view of the data stored in BookKeeper. One thing that I hope was not lost in this appendix is the amount of administrative burden placed on operators of geo-replicated clusters. While the barrier to entry is lower than many other systems, it is much higher than managing a Pulsar cluster in a single region. The best way to get accustomed to geo-replication is practice. Tools like Kind make it easy to set up multiple Kubernetes clusters locally that you can use for replicating multiple regions. Additionally, using cloud platforms like AWS and Google Cloud offers the opportunity to deploy across multiple regions without much additional configuration.

Security, Authentication, and Authorization in Pulsar

In this book, all of the code snippets share two qualities:

- There is no encryption.
- There is no authentication or authorization.

While operating a real cluster requires good authorization and authentication practices, it was not a wholly necessary requirement to enable these features for pedagogy. I thought it would be appropriate to include some details about security in Pulsar in an appendix where I could introduce some new topics in an environment that was isolated from the rest of our learning. In this appendix you'll learn about:

- Encryption in transit
- Encryption at rest
- Authentication
- Authorization

Encryption in Transit

Encryption in transit is ensuring that data traveling over the internet is encrypted. This means that if the data were collected in transit, it could not be read by the interceptor (see Figure D-1). Encryption in transit is enabled by encrypting the messages before sending them over the wire. In Pulsar you can do that with the following:

```
PulsarClient pulsarClient = PulsarClient.builder()
        .serviceUrl("pulsar://localhost:6650")
```

```
        .build();

Producer producer = pulsarClient.newProducer()
            .topic("persistent://my-tenant/my-ns/my-topic")
            .addEncryptionKey("myappkey")
            .cryptoKeyReader(new RawFileKeyReader("test_ecdsa_pubkey.pem",
              "test_ecdsa_privkey.pem"))
            .create();
```

It uses a public/private key pair for the encryption.

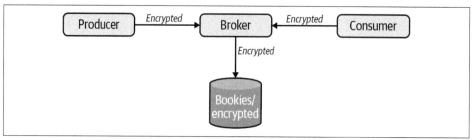

Figure D-1. Encryption in transit in the Pulsar topology uses public/private key pairs for the encryption.

Encryption at Rest

In Pulsar, we want to encrypt the data in transit and at rest so that only someone with the correct private keys can decrypt messages. In Pulsar, if the data is encrypted by the client, the broker will store the message in BookKeeper encrypted as well. Figure D-2 provides an illustration of TLS encryption on messages being published and consumed.

To ensure that data is encrypted with TLS, we can create a client that uses a certificate:

```
import org.apache.pulsar.client.api.PulsarClient;

PulsarClient client = PulsarClient.builder()
    .serviceUrl("pulsar+ssl://broker.example.com:6651/")
    .enableTls(true)
    .tlsTrustCertsFilePath("/path/to/ca.cert.pem")
    .enableTlsHostnameVerification(false)
    .allowTlsInsecureConnection(false)
    .build();
```

Figure D-2. Trust certificates are used to encrypt messages.

Authentication

Authentication is the process of asking an entity to prove they are who they say they are via credentials. Authentication can take on many forms, including the following:

- Username/password authentication
- Key authentication
- Alternative factor authentication
- SMS authentication

In Pulsar, authentication is used to ensure that clients are who they say they are, and that identity is associated with their authorization. Figure D-3 shows how token-based authentication works, as producers and consumers share their tokens to authenticate with the cluster.

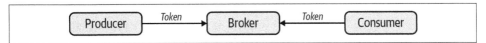

Figure D-3. In token-based authentication, producers and consumers share their tokens to authenticate with the cluster.

Here is an example of a client using token-based authentication:

```
PulsarClient client = PulsarClient.builder()
    .serviceUrl("pulsar://broker.example.com:6650/")
    .authentication(

AuthenticationFactory.token("eyJhbGciOiJIUzI1NiJ9.eyJzdWIiOiJKb2UifQ.ipevRNuRP6H
flG8cFKnmUPtypruRC4fb1DWtoLL62SY")
    .build();
```

The client uses JSON Web Tokens (JWT) to authenticate with the broker.

Authorization

Authorization is the privilege of performing actions on given resources. In Pulsar, authorization is used to ensure that an entity can perform actions like creating topics, administering to namespaces, and creating geo-replications. Figure D-4 depicts the authorization model in Pulsar. At the top are superusers who can create clusters and geo-replication policies. They can also create tenant admins. Tenant admins can perform actions like creating and managing namespace and tenant policies as well as granting permissions to clients. Clients can create consumers and producers and manage their configurations.

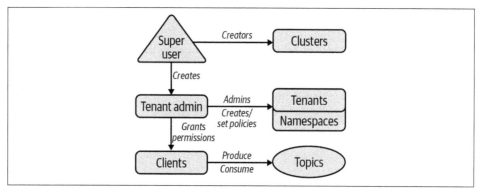

Figure D-4. Superusers can create clusters, geo-replication policies, and tenant admins. Clients can create consumers and producers and manage their configurations.

Summary

Authentication and authorization are critical in making Pulsar safe and usable by large organizations. It organizes the cluster users and ensures that data is safe in transit and at rest. I'm not a security engineer by trade, and every time I get involved with encryption, authentication, and authorization, I get overwhelmed and a little uncertain about my skills. I think many UX improvements can be made in this space to make authentication and authorization much easier. I should not have to generate any certificates.

Index

About the Author

Jowanza Joseph is a staff software engineer at Finicity. Jowanza leads the development of Finicity's Open Banking Event Mesh. Jowanza has worked on streaming and messaging technologies for close to a decade. Prior to Finicity, Jowanza worked on the Streaming Data Platform at Pluralsight, working with Apache Kafka, Akka, and Kubernetes at scale. Earlier, he worked with Apache Pulsar, using Pulsar to build a fully managed messaging and stream processing platform, processing billions of messages per day. With his passion for distributed systems and messaging systems, Jowanza writes about these topics on his blog. Jowanza is also an avid public speaker. Over the years, he has given talks on Apache Pulsar and other topics at Strange Loop, Abstractions, Strata O'Reilly Conference, Open Source Summit, and The Lead Dev.

Colophon

The animal on the cover of *Mastering Apache Pulsar* is a pompadour cotinga (*Xipholena punicea*), a species of bird found in northern South America, particularly the rainforest canopies of Brazil, Colombia, Venezuela, and the Guianas, and the white sand forests of northern Peru.

All cotingas have broad, hooked bills, round wings, and legs built for perching, but the males of this species have a distinct burgundy head and body, bright white, black-tipped wings, and yellow eyes. Females lack the red-wine plumage, having a more subtle pale grey head and body, thought to provide better camouflage when nesting and looking after young.

The treetop habitat and remote distribution of pompadour cotingas make this bird difficult to observe, although ornithologists have found that, during the mating season, males are known to perform elaborate chasing rituals to display dominance to a female who will then raise the young alone.

While currently listed with a status of Least Concern by the IUCN, the deforestation of the Amazon rainforest will eliminate a significant portion of the pompadour cotinga's habitat. Many of the animals on O'Reilly covers are endangered; all of them are important to the world.

The cover illustration is by Karen Montgomery, based on a black and white engraving from *Birds and Beasts*. The cover fonts are Gilroy Semibold and Guardian Sans. The text font is Adobe Minion Pro; the heading font is Adobe Myriad Condensed; and the code font is Dalton Maag's Ubuntu Mono.

O'REILLY®

There's much more where this came from.

Experience books, videos, live online training courses, and more from O'Reilly and our 200+ partners—all in one place.

Learn more at oreilly.com/online-learning

Milton Keynes UK
Ingram Content Group UK Ltd.
UKHW020833260624
444734UK00007B/348